1001 Ways you can save the Planet

D0767010

1001

Ways you can save the Planet

Practical ideas to heal and change the world

JOANNA YARROW

BEYOND GREEN LTD

DUNCAN BAIRD PUBLISHERS
LONDON

1001 Ways You Can Save the Planet Joanna Yarrow

First published in the United Kingdom and Ireland
in 2007 by Duncan Baird Publishers Ltd
Sixth Floor, Castle House, 75–76 Wells Street,
London W1T 3QH

Conceived and created by Duncan Baird Publishers

Editor: James Hodgson
Managing Designer: Suzanne Tuhrim
Managing Editor: Christopher Westhorp
Commissioned artwork: Andrew Selby

British Library Cataloguing-in-Publication Data: A CIP
record for this book is available from the British Library

ISBN: 978-1-84483-376-4

10 9 8 7 6 5 4 3

Typeset in AT Shannon
Colour reproduction by Scanhouse, Malaysia
Printed in Singapore by Imago

Publisher's Note: This book is printed using mineral
oil-free vegetable-based inks on paper produced from
pulp obtained from sustainably managed forests, and
from paper mills that meet environmental standard ISO
14001. It's 100 per cent recyclable – not that you'll
ever want to let your copy go …

How can I help to protect the rainforest – the lungs of the planet?

What arguments should I use to persuade my friends to recycle waste?

What can one citizen do to help protect the ozone layer?

1001 WAYS YOU CAN SAVE THE PLANET

Is nuclear power a threat to our world or the answer to its problems?

How can I conserve energy around the home – and save money at the same time?

How can I help to ensure the best possible legacy for my grandchildren – a habitable world?

Would it really make a difference if I walked more, or caught the bus or train, and drove less?

Do my shopping and eating habits affect the health of the planet?

INTRODUCTION

Unless you've spent the last few years living on a desert island or mountain top, you'll probably have noticed that our planet seems to be in trouble. But however much you care, it can be hard to know how to help when you're already leading a busy life. This book is designed to inspire and guide anyone who wants to play an active part in caring for the environment, but who's at a loss about where to start.

The state of the environment was once a fringe discussion. A well-publicized campaign to save a cuddly jungle animal or pretty piece of land in our neighbourhood might have caught our attention occasionally, but it was easy to dismiss eco warriors and worriers as well-meaning "alternative" types, whose concerns over the fate of a few obscure beetles and far-flung swamps had no bearing on the lives of anyone else. Nature seemed so resilient, the globe so large, and scientists so clever that it was hard to imagine our lifestyles could really dent its web of life in any significant way.

But times have changed fast, and the frighteningly perilous state of the Earth is now mainstream news. Evidence from around the world shows that a small number of the Earth's inhabitants (we humans) are causing irreversible damage to the planet, pushing its support systems out of kilter and jeopardizing the future of all the other species we share it with.

Our destructive impact is evident in every part of the globe. For example, fish are changing sex as a result of exposure to man-made toxins, and species are becoming extinct at the fastest rate in history as their habitats are destroyed. Climate change associated with the burning of fossil fuels brings its own tales of woe – from the drowning or starving of polar bears as the ice they hunt on melts earlier each year, to the threat posed to the homes of hundreds of millions of people by rising sea levels.

These are no longer problems that our grandchildren might have to deal with if they're unlucky. They're happening now and happening fast. Many scientists predict that unless we significantly reduce our impact on the environment, within the next couple of decades we'll pass a tipping point where runaway climate change is unleashed – a point beyond which the planet will change irreversibly, whatever we do.

Fundamentally, the planet itself will be fine. It has weathered many changes, and – perhaps short of complete nuclear holocaust – it will weather whatever we throw at it. But it won't necessarily survive the onslaught we're currently subjecting it to in a condition that's comfortable – or even endurable – for the human species.

These problems can seem very distant from the reality of our everyday lives. When you've got to get the kids to school, pay the mortgage, fit in a hair appointment, get the garden sorted out, write a work report and visit the in-laws, saving the planet can seem like one chore too many.

But you don't necessarily need extra time or money, a cape, underwear worn as outerwear or any special powers to do your bit to look after the planet. The damage we're wreaking is a direct result of the way we choose to live our lives. Pretty much everything we do has an impact on the natural world. So changes to any of our daily activities, from the moment we get up in the morning until we go to bed at night (hopefully between organic cotton sheets), represent an opportunity to look after the planet better without adding too much to our "to do" list. Anything, from the food we eat and the way we store and cook it to the way we get to work and the work we do, our shopping habits, the clothes we wear and the way we launder them, the way we wash, play sport and entertain ourselves, and how we maintain our home, can be changed in simple but significant ways for the benefit of the planet.

You don't need to be a paragon of virtue to make a difference. There's something in planet care for even the most selfish of us. And there are side benefits, including saving money, losing weight, getting fitter, keeping your kids amused, outdoing your neighbours or simply fostering a warm inner glow.

Prioritizing the planet is a mindset you can apply to everything you do, from planning a party to planning your retirement, getting drunk to getting a mortgage. Excitingly, as the challenges of living sustainably become more apparent, people and organizations around the world are responding with a range of creative actions, innovations and initiatives from the tiny to the colossal.

This book contains an eclectic mix of ways you could help to protect and enhance the planet and develop a more just and equitable society for everyone living on it. Some are tiny modifications in personal habits, which, repeated daily, could have a huge impact over a lifetime. Others are inspiring ideas for longer-term lifestyle choices, which require bigger commitment or investment. You will also find discussions of key environmental issues, such as climate change, GMO foods and renewable energy sources. There's no single recipe for a perfectly planet-friendly life, but there are definitely more than 1,001 positive actions you can add to the mix …

Whether you dip into it for occasional inspiration or read it from cover to cover, I hope that this book will stop you feeling that there's nothing you can do to help look after this wonderful planet. Find the suggestions you like, incorporate them into a personalized programme of lifestyle changes, and let's live on the Earth as if we intended to stay!

Joanna Yarrow, Beyond Green (www.beyondgreen.co.uk)

1   **Offset your flight's CO$_2$** Aviation may soon account for 15 per cent of all greenhouse gas emissions. When there's no alternative to flying, why not help mitigate the environmental costs? Specialist companies (see page 370) allow you to calculate online your seat's proportion of the flight's emissions and negate it by buying "offsets" – a contribution they invest in CO$_2$ (carbon dioxide) reduction measures, such as planting trees. On a return flight between New York and London your 1.5 tonnes of CO$_2$ incurs a $15 offset.

2   **SPEAK UP** If you see something you think might be pollution – from rubbish dumped in a park to foamy scum on the surface of a river – notify your local authority or environment agency. Perhaps someone else has already pointed it out, but it's far better for the problem to be reported twice than not at all.

3   **Lusher lawns** Longer grass retains moisture better than short turf, so in the summer let your lawn grow to at least 4cm before you cut it to avoid brown patches and unnecessary watering.

4. **BUY SOFTWOOD** Does your furniture need to be made out of a rare, slow-growing hardwood when you could use attractive, fast-growing (and so more readily renewable) spruce, larch or pine?

---

5. **Extremely cool** Keep a jug or bottle of tap water in the fridge. This will mean that you don't waste water waiting for it to run cold from the tap.

6. **Donate your weekend shave** Save on water, foam and balm by forgoing your daily shaving ritual at the weekend. Your partner might object to your stubble, but just remind them, it's all for the greater good ...

7. **Don't be floored by choices** Rather than artificial fibres, choose natural floor coverings such as sisal, jute, coir or cork.

8. **Keep pet birds exotic** Colourful parrots, macaws and other birds are better off left in their natural environment rather than being dragooned as domestic pets. Undermine trapping

and trafficking by not buying. Instead, save for a vacation to the rainforest – setting aside enough to offset your flight's CO_2 emissions (see page 12), of course. There you can see birds flying in their natural habitat, and your money will help to support local communities trying to keep things that way.

9   **Wonderful baking soda** Forget fancy cleaning products: they're expensive and we need contact with some of the germs they obliterate to keep our natural defences ticking over. Use cheap and effective baking soda as an all-purpose cleaner, scouring powder, polish and fungicide. And with what's left, do some baking.

10   **Wake up and smell the coffee** Shun chemical-containing "air fresheners" and make use of naturally satisfying aromas, such as pot pourri – or fresh bread and coffee!

11   **Read all about it** Newspaper is one of the easiest materials to recycle. Every time you recycle a pile of papers a metre high, you save a tree from the chop.

12   Be a beekeeper The humble bee is a real friend to humankind, not only because it generates honey and wax but also because it pollinates wild flowers, garden plants and crops that would otherwise become extinct. Indeed, it's been estimated that without these buzzy insects the planet would last for only 60 years. By cultivating a small "hobby hive" we can support bees in their vital work – it requires only about half an hour's work per week to produce jars and jars of delicious, home-grown honey.

13 **Cut your carbs** Carbon dioxide (CO_2) is an essential component of life on Earth. It traps some of the sun's rays in the atmosphere, warming the planet to a habitable temperature. But human activity – particularly the burning of fossil fuels – is raising the amount of CO_2 in the atmosphere to a level higher than at any time in the last 650,000 years. It's acting like a blanket that's too thick, warming the Earth to a degree that could fundamentally alter the climatic balance that allows life as we know it to flourish.

All manner of activities – from breathing to driving cars – produce CO_2. The average person in the UK generates around 11 tonnes, and the average American 20 tonnes, per year, from all activities. If we're to limit climate change, scientists estimate that we each need to reduce our so-called "carbon footprint" to less than 2.5 tonnes per year. That may sound draconian, but it's achievable through a series of lifestyle changes.

Visit an online carbon-footprint calculator (see page 370) to **find out how much CO_2 you're producing per year (14)** and follow the suggestions in this book to curb your carbon habit. **Resubmit your details every few months (15)** and watch the kilos drop off your annual emissions as you change your habits.

16   **Water torture** There's no point heating water to near boiling for washing as you'll just have to mix it with cold, unless you're a fan of the boiled lobster look. So save energy by lowering your water-heater thermostat to about 60 degrees Celsius.

17   **Worship the sun** Make the most of the sun's warmth in even the coldest climates by using the sunniest rooms in your house more during winter. When it's time to repaint the exterior of your house, **choose a dark colour to absorb more heat (18)**.

19   **Keep in tune** Have your boiler and gas fire serviced annually – both for safety and to ensure that they're performing as efficiently as possible.

When regular servicing's no longer enough and you need to get a new boiler, **invest in a super-efficient gas condensing model (20)**, which could use up to 30 per cent less energy than your existing boiler.

21   **Directional heating** If your heating system uses radiators, make sure you're heating your rooms rather than your walls by fitting reflective material such as aluminium foil behind them.

Another approach is to **fit a shelf a couple of inches above a radiator (22)** to guide the heat into the room rather than up the wall.

---

23   **BLESSED RELEASE** Bleed your radiators regularly to remove any trapped air and ensure they're working at maximum efficiency.

---

24   **Under wraps** In colder climates up to half the heat used in the home is lost through exterior walls. If you have cavity walls, you can keep your home snug by having insulating material injected into the cavities through a small hole in each wall. Solid walls can be insulated by adding a layer of cladding material.

Installing loft insulation (25) is a straightforward and cost-effective way to minimize your heating bills and cut your home's CO_2 emissions. To be most effective, the insulating layer should be at least 18cm thick.

Whether insulating your walls or your loft, try to **use a recycled or environmentally benign insulating material (26)**, made from, for example, recycled newspaper, sheep's wool or cellulose fibre.

27 **Thrive in an urban jungle** Modern furniture and electronic equipment can emit enough chemicals to make the air in our homes and offices more hazardous than the air outdoors. Some plants are particularly effective absorbers of these harmful pollutants – clean up the air indoors and brighten your work and living space by surrounding yourself with peace lilies, spider plants, Boston ferns, rubber plants and palms.

28 **Beyond fossil fuel** By 2030, global energy demand is projected to be two-thirds higher than it is today. Relying solely on fossil fuels isn't an option: reserves are finite; the potential damage to the environment, infinite.

Renewable energy sources, such as wind, wave and solar power, are an increasingly viable alternative. Apart from being carbon-neutral (emitting negligible CO_2 into the atmosphere), they offer numerous other advantages. For example, they rely on free fuel, so running costs are minimal, avoiding the economic chaos that fuel price fluctuations can cause. They are also far less vulnerable to terrorist attack than conventional energy sources.

Renewable resources currently provide only a small share of global energy production, but wind and solar power are the fastest-growing energy sources in the world. The costs of these and other renewables are falling rapidly as technologies become more advanced, manufacturing is automated, and economies of scale are achieved through increased production volumes.

If progress continues at the current rate, up to a billion people could be served with renewable energy in the next decade, and renewables could account for a third to a half of world energy production by 2050.

29 **Words of encouragement** If you're feeling sad, apathetic, empty, afraid, angry or guilty about the state of the world, the healing work of the American eco-philosopher, facilitator and activist Joanna Macy may help inspire you to action. In books such as *Coming Back to Life*, she shares tried and tested practices for reconnecting ourselves to the natural world.

---

30 **THE WISDOM OF CHILDREN** Encourage children you know to write poetry about the wonders of nature, and help them to create a poetry tree with their poems on paper leaves.

---

31 **Stub it out** Tobacco growing involves heavy pesticide and herbicide use. Much of this toxic sludge ends up in the soil and in waterways, causing significant environmental damage in some of the world's poorest countries. The rest ends up in your lungs.

32 **No time to spare** Play an active role in protecting the web of life that supports us all by getting involved in a conservation project. You could go it alone by creating some new habitats in your garden, or join in a bigger project run by a conservation organization (see page 370). Ideally do both – the Millennium Ecosystem Assessment estimates that 10–30 per cent of species are under serious threat, so we need to get our skates on.

33 **Don't get palmed off** Palm oil is found in many products, from face creams to margarines. While it may impart a smooth texture, its production gives ecosystems a rough ride. Palm plantations are replacing huge swathes of ecologically valuable Indonesian forests and their inhabitants (including the last few orang-utans and Sumatran tigers). So look for products containing less destructive plant oils, such as canola, sunflower or olive.

34 **Crumb-free keyboard** When you're at work and need to go out to buy lunch, relax and eat your food in a café rather than taking it back to your desk – you won't need to use any packaging, and you'll be more relaxed when you get back to the office.

35 **Be a smart cook** Cooking meals from scratch is a healthier, more energy-efficient option than buying processed food or takeaways, but you can save even more energy by not being a slave to the cookbook. For example, if you **turn the oven off ten minutes before the time stated in the recipe (36)**, the residual heat will keep the food cooking. Similarly, **don't bother preheating the oven (37)** unless you're cooking pastries, bread or a soufflé.

38 **Less speed, more fuel** Attention all speed freaks! Driving at 50mph is 25 per cent more fuel-efficient than driving at 70mph. And you're much less likely to wrap your car around a tree.

39 **Say what you need** Whether it be your milkman or the manager of your local convenience store, people will be more likely to offer you the service you want if they know what you're looking for. So be sure to ask manufacturers and retailers to provide goods and services that help you in your mission to go green.

40 **Naturally lighter** Help your home to work in harmony with sunshine. By painting interior walls in pale colours and keeping your windows clean, you'll make your rooms look brighter and reduce the need for artificial light.

41 **VIRTUOUS CYCLE** Teach a child to ride a bicycle and set them up with a healthy, eco-friendly, economical habit for life. Every four-mile trip by bike rather than car prevents around 7kg of air pollution, and builds a strong heart – frequent cyclists are as fit as people ten years younger who don't do regular exercise.

42 **Under pressure** Turbo-charge the cooking process by using a pressure cooker, which will cut cooking times and should use 50–75 per cent less energy than a normal saucepan.

43 **Keep it sealed** Covering food (or ice cubes) in your fridge or freezer (ideally with a lid or plate rather than foil or cling film) not only stops the food drying out, but prevents the moisture it contains condensing as ice on the walls of the appliance. A fridge or freezer with iced-up walls uses more energy and needs defrosting more often.

44 **Cold facts** Fridges and freezers are probably the most expensive electrical items to run in our homes, so make sure they're not using more energy than they need to. Next time you have to buy a new one, **choose the most energy-efficient model (45)** you can find. You'll recoup your investment in saved energy during the first few years of the machine's life.

Whatever the age of your appliance, don't make it work harder than it needs to. **Regulate the internal temperature (46)**: fridges don't need to be colder than 3–5 degrees Celsius and freezers should operate at minus 15 degrees. Invest in fridge and freezer thermometers if your appliances don't have them built in. To improve efficiency **clean dust off the coils (47)** at the back of your fridge or freezer and **defrost regularly (48)** – when the ice is 3–5mm thick. **Install your fridge and freezer in a cool spot (49)**, well away from the cooker, boiler and radiators, with a gap behind of at least 6cm for air to circulate. **Check that the door seal is tight (50)** by putting a piece of paper in the door: if the paper slips out when the door's closed, you may need to change the seal to prevent cold air from escaping. **Wait for cooked food to cool (51)** before you put it in the fridge, and **don't leave the door open for longer than necessary (52)** – it's only your food that needs refrigerating, not your kitchen.

53 **Try a Savaplug®** This ingenious gadget only allows power through to your fridge or freezer in short bursts as required, rather than in the continuous flow that makes these appliances such voracious consumers of energy. Some modern fridges have integrated this technology, but on other models – particularly older ones – fitting a Savaplug® can reduce energy consumption by as much as 20 per cent.

54 **Put mothballs into mothballs** The distinctive smell of mothballs comes from the evaporation of their toxic chemical ingredients, naphthalene and dichlorobenzene, which are both bio-accumulative. Instead of noxious-smelling balls, why not use a natural moth-repellant? Add to your wardrobe and drawers cedar disks, lavender bags or a mix of herbs and spices such as rosemary, cinnamon, cardamom and cloves to keep moths at bay the sweet-smelling way.

55 **A more seductive candlelight** Traditional paraffin-wax candles are petroleum-based. Once lit, they emit toxins such as acetone, benzene, lead and mercury into the air. Beeswax and soy candles, by contrast, are toxin-free. Not only do they provide a healthier atmosphere for romantic dinners for two, but the pleasant experience will last longer, as these natural candles burn for 50 per cent longer than synthetic ones.

56 **Plastic not so fantastic** When buying presents for children, steer clear of toys made from PVC, which can leach noxious chemicals when the surface is scratched, and emits carcinogenic toxins if burnt. Toys that don't contain this harmful form of plastic are labelled "PVC-free". Better still, try to **find toys made from materials such as wood or fabric (57)**, which can be just as appealing to kids. Try also to **avoid toys that need batteries (58)**, which are energy-intensive and can leak toxins when trashed. Get yourself a set of rechargeable batteries and a charger (ideally solar) to run any electric items your children can't do without.

59 **Think bigger** Try translating some of the changes you're making in your personal life into other contexts. Let people at your workplace, school, place of worship or favourite shop know what you're up to. They may want to get involved, which will help you to make a much greater impact.

60 **Eat slowly** Take time to enjoy the whole process of preparing
and eating food in ways that have developed over centuries.
Become part of the international Slow Food movement, which
aims to "promote gastronomic culture, develop a taste education,
conserve agricultural biodiversity and protect traditional foods
at risk of extinction."

61 **Less is more** It requires much more land, water and energy
to derive food from animals than from vegetables. For example,
in the USA it takes 140 litres of water to produce a kilogram of
wheat, but a whopping 4,400 litres to produce a kilogram of
beef. If life without steak and chips sounds just too bleak, try
cutting down your meat consumption to one or two meals each
week, and use the money you've saved to splash out on locally
raised, organic meat specialities.

62 **Glug down some organic milk** If you're trying
to "go organic", milk is a good place to start.
The price difference is marginal, but the
health benefits are significant: organic
milk contains much higher levels of

nutrients – for example, up to two-thirds more omega 3 essential fatty acids – than intensively farmed milk.

63   **My darling turpentine** Next time you've got paintbrushes to clean, use real turpentine instead of turps substitute or white spirit. It's distilled from pine and so smells delicious. And, most importantly for the health of those around you, it's low in volatile organic compounds (see page 186).

64   **Genuine article** Choose real corks rather than plastic ones. Not only are they easier to get out of the bottle, but they're made from a renewable resource, grown in forests that support a huge variety of wildlife, including endangered species, such as the Iberian lynx. And when you've finished with them you can collect them to use as firelighters or put them on your compost heap.

65   **Little by little** If you try to take on too many of the suggestions in this book at once, you may end up doing most of them only a few times before lapsing. To avoid eco-evangelist burnout, try to add a few of your favourite suggestions to your routine each week and build up your portfolio of lifestyle changes gradually.

66 **Commune with peers** If you've got a good idea you'd like to share, if you need something, or if you've got something to offer, put a notice up in the local shops, or on your community website.

---

67 **EVERY DAY IS BOXING DAY** A bored child can be brought to life by a simple cardboard box, which a fertile imagination can turn into anything from a den to a spaceship. Before you recycle the box, let your child have hours or even days of fun with it.

68 **Know your plastics** Plastic comes in many different forms, and each type must be recycled separately. The only way of sorting plastics is by hand, so do your bit by acquainting yourself with the identifying code numbers for different types of plastic, which are usually embossed within a mobius loop symbol, choosing the types that are most easily recyclable, such as PET (code number 1) and HDPE (code number 2), and putting them into the appropriate recycling system when you've finished with them.

69 **Nappy talk** Your little darling's likely to plough through around 5,000 nappies before he or she is potty-trained. If you use disposables, that's about a tonne of nappies to landfill on baby's behalf. So try reusable nappies – modern ones are surprisingly streamlined. Using reusables will save you a huge amount of cash. So if you find the laundering process an unpleasant chore, why not spend some of the money you've saved on **subscribing to a local nappy service (70)**? They'll provide a constant supply of clean cloth nappies and collect the used ones from your home. Their large-scale laundry process is also more efficient than washing at home.

However, when you're away from home, reusable nappies may not be practical. For road trips, **use disposable nappies made from recycled materials (71)**. Check that they don't contain latex, perfumes, gels or dyes. Such synthetic ingredients can be toxic when absorbed into babies' delicate skin, and cause pollution when buried or incinerated. Certain brands are fully biodegradable, so you can put them on a compost heap!

72   **Don't wipe out your savings** The nappy isn't the only area of baby care to have been invaded by throwaway products. Disposable baby wipes are also rife, but you can easily do without them by using washable wipes – either bought or home made from old material. You'll save a pile of money and a mountain of waste, and protect your child and the environment from the synthetic chemicals found in many disposable wipes.

73   **Children's menu** Make your own baby food using locally grown or home-grown organic fruit and vegetables. A batch of pureed fruit and veg frozen in small containers will last for ages. It will be fresher, cheaper, tastier and more nutritious than shop-bought versions, and quick and easy to make.

74   **Happy-flappy** Butterflies and moths are becoming ever rarer as their habitats are destroyed by agriculture and other human activity. Do your bit to redress the balance by planting butterfly-friendly flowering plants such as lilac, buddleia, honeysuckle and evening primrose, and enjoy the colour that the flowers and butterflies bring to your garden.

75   **Breast is best** Not all mothers are able to breastfeed, but if it's an option, breast milk is not only healthier for your baby, but much healthier for the environment. It comes without any packaging, and doesn't require fossil fuel energy to make it!

If breastfeeding isn't possible, **choose organic baby formula (76)**. That way, you won't be feeding your baby the traces of antibiotics, pesticides and fertilizer often found in non-organic versions.

77   **Choose a shortlived casket** Your coffin is one thing that doesn't need to be built to last! Cardboard or wicker coffins decompose quickly into the soil. Ask for one in your will and make your loved ones aware of your wishes.

78   **Mi casa, tu casa** Whether you like to experience different cultures on the road or in the comfort of your own living room, consider joining SERVAS (www.servas.org), an international peace organization that fosters networks of hosts and travellers, encouraging personal contacts between people from different parts of the world.

---

79   **A PLACE OF YOUR OWN** Find a "magic spot" in a patch of nature (however small) and return there regularly, whenever you need space to reflect.

---

80   **Buzz off** Keep flies away naturally with essential oils such as citronella, mint, eucalyptus and clove.

---

81   **Thoughts at the checkout** Ask yourself whether the item you're about to buy is something you really need. Will it make you more fulfilled? If not, try doing something else to nurture yourself instead, like eating good food, doing something special with a friend, going for a walk, or planning something you've been interested in for ages.

82　**Cut down your wine miles** As you'll know if
you've ever lugged a case back from the off-
licence, bottles of wine take some carrying. So,
minimize your contribution to the environmental
headache of hauling this heavy treat around the globe
by favouring wines produced as close to home as possible.

83　**Dressed for warmth** Give your hot water cylinder a cosy jacket
if it hasn't got one already. That way, more heat will get into your
shower and less will escape into your airing cupboard.

84　**Piping hot** Make sure water inside pipes stays hot – particularly
during long trips through cold areas such as the garage – by
wrapping any exposed pipework in insulating material.

85　**Decondition yourself** Minimize your dependence on energy-
hungry air conditioning by tackling heat the natural way. **Shade
sunny windows (86)** with curtains and blinds inside, and trees
and climbing plants outside. **Open windows at night (87)**
to allow cross-ventilation, but keep them shut during the day.
Install a large fan in the attic (88) and run it in the evening

with windows and loft hatch open to pull cooler air into the house and hot air into the roof space.

If you must use air conditioning, go for a low energy-rated system (89) and make sure all the ducts are properly sealed. And use it only when it's really necessary!

90   **Window-wise** A large proportion of a building's heat can be lost through its windows. You can minimize this waste by installing double glazing, ideally using low-emissivity glass, which further limits heat loss. If that's too big a project, **fix insulating film (91)** over each pane to achieve a similar (although less perfectly transparent) effect for a fraction of the price.

92   **Curtain magic** Not only do curtains or blinds create a cosy atmosphere, but they can be as effective at keeping warmth in as an extra layer of glazing – particularly if they have thick thermal linings. To keep rooms warm during winter, **close curtains and blinds just before dusk (93)**, and open them in the morning to let the sun's heat into your home during the day. And to keep rooms cool during summer, leave curtains and blinds closed during the day and open them in the evening.

94 Walk the bus to school The school run can cause major congestion problems, contributes to pollution and deprives children of valuable exercise. If there's no school bus service and you can't walk your own kids to school each day, you could get together with other parents in your neighbourhood to organize a "walking bus" – a scheme where trained adults collect children along a set route and supervise their walk to school.

95 Little helpers Put your children in charge of some green tasks around the home – such as checking that lights and appliances are switched off, looking after the composting or feeding the birds – and reward them for doing well. Find something they enjoy and the habits are likely to last a lifetime.

96 **Dematerialize your child's school** Ask the staff to match your green efforts at home by cutting back on energy and waste on campus. **Getting rid of vending machines (97)** stocked with canned drinks and overpackaged snacks is a good place to start.

98 **Give it like you mean it** Make a friend a present out of something significant to you – perhaps a book from your collection that you have read and particularly enjoyed. Or **devote time to make a gift (99)**: bake a cake or frame some photos of a happy time you've spent together.

100 **Eat before you shop** It's frightening how much food the average household throws away. Studies show we buy more food if we shop when hungry. So a good meal before you hit the shops, combined with a proper shopping list, helps you to buy only what you need, and reduce this wasteful, expensive and (ultimately) smelly food glut.

101   **Natural deterrents** Slugs and snails are some of the most destructive invaders the average gardener has to deal with. Fortunately, there are numerous harmless alternatives to chemical pellets, which should be avoided as they kill not only the pests but also beneficial creatures, such as hedgehogs. Slugs and snails like damp conditions, so you can **protect vulnerable plants with a mulch of rough material (102)**, such as sand, gravel or even crunched-up eggshells. These greedy gastropods are also deterred by copper, which gives them a mild electric shock: to steer them away from container plants, **attach a ribbon of copper tape (103)**, at least 5cm wide, around the pot.

The simplest – and perhaps most effective – way to deprive slugs and snails of a damp dining environment is to **water your plants first thing in the morning (104)** rather than in the evening when your unwanted guests are at their most active.

105   **Labour and energy saving** Running a dishwasher can actually have less impact on the environment than doing dishes by hand if you choose a water- and energy-efficient model and put it on only when there's a full load, using a low-temperature setting and eco-friendly dishwasher powder or tablets. Also, it's not necessary to pre-rinse items unless they're covered with burnt-on or dried-on food. For sustained efficiency **regularly clean the filter (106)** at the bottom of the machine and **prevent limescale build-up (107)** by keeping the salt level topped up.

108   **Saline solution** Rather than using a commercial product, use salt to draw out red wine and fruit juice stains.

109   **Distraction tactics** As well as creating a barrier around the plants you don't want slugs and snails to attack (see opposite), you can also tempt them away by setting bait. **Leave uprooted weeds out in a pile (110)** in a damp corner of the garden rather than putting them straight on the compost heap: slugs and snails like to feed on wilted leaves, which are softer than those on living plants. However, **avoid using beer traps (111)** – small containers of beer buried in the soil. They will attract not only their intended targets to meet a boozy end but also useful creatures, including ground beetles, which actually prey on slugs. And, of course, they're a waste of good beer!

112   **IN TUNE WITH TUNA** High consumer demand means that tuna are being endangered by commercial overfishing. If you're keen to benefit from the fish's health-giving properties, rather than cutting it out entirely, try only buying rod- and line-caught skipjack tuna. These stocks are not threatened by overfishing and the fishing method avoids killing the huge numbers of other small fish that are caught in commercial nets.

---

113   **Count your cuppas** Pots, watched or otherwise, boil much faster if you put only as much water in them as you need. Boiling one cup of water rather than a full kettle saves enough electricity to power an energy-saving lightbulb for nine hours. If you find it hard to judge the water level, **use a cup or mug to fill the kettle (114)** with the required number of "portions" of water.

115   **Hot pot** Once food's cooked there's no need to leave the stove on to keep it warm. A few teatowels on the pan's lid will keep the food inside piping hot for quite a while.

116   **Clean your kettle** Keeping your kettle free from limescale makes it more efficient, producing quicker, lower-energy cups of tea – and they'll taste better too. Try boiling two cups of white vinegar diluted in a little water to dislodge calcium deposits. Remember to rinse it out before your next brew!

117   **Screensaver** Make a point of switching off your computer screen each time you leave your desk, especially for longer periods such as your lunchbreak. A computer in "screensaver" mode uses almost as much energy as it does when it's being used, and, frankly, even the most profound (or profane) of scrolling messages doesn't add that much to office life.

118   **A slow thaw** Plan ahead so you don't need to use a microwave to defrost frozen food. Ideally, let the food thaw in the fridge overnight – its chilliness will leave less work for the fridge to do.

119   **Human radiators** When you host a party, take advantage of the heat generated by your guests to turn the central heating down.

120 **Smart planting** For chemical-free gardening success, work with mother nature rather than trying to defy her. **Choose naturally pest-resistant varieties of plants (121)** and, when deciding where to position them, **take account of the type of soil and amount of sun and moisture that suit them best (122)**. If they're in the right conditions, they'll grow strong and be better able to defend themselves against pests and disease. To give additional protection, you could **try companion planting (123)**. This involves mixing together plants that provide useful nutrients for each other or attract predators to prey on the other's pests – for example, tomatoes with carrots, garlic with roses, or nasturtiums with pumpkins, cucumbers and squash.

124 **Patio heater? Pah!** If you want to invest in some garden hardware, make sure it doesn't cost the Earth. One of the most short-sighted fads of recent years, the gas-fired patio heater wastes energy and produces copious amounts of pollution. Keep warm with extra layers, and a wood-fired brazier or chiminea if you're still cold.

125 **The lights are on ...** Turning off the light when you leave a room is a very easy and obvious way of saving energy, but a surprising number of empty rooms and even whole buildings blaze with light at night. One way to stop this happening is to **fit movement sensors (126)** so that lights are activated only when they're needed – including those in domestic outdoor areas.

127 **Bright idea** Switching to compact fluorescent lightbulbs (CFLs) has never been easier, as shapes and sizes are now available to fit most light fittings. Each bulb uses only about a quarter the electricity of a normal one and they last up to ten times longer, saving you loads of money and energy (as well as the hassle of replacing dead lightbulbs on a regular basis).

128 **Clear as day** Before switching on electric lights, make sure you're making the most of natural daylight. Move your desk near a window – but try not to get distracted by the view!

129 **A question of timing** There's no point heating your home when you're out or asleep, so set the timer to switch the heating on only when you're home and awake. If you haven't got a timer, get one fitted – the investment will be paid back in weeks.

130 **Bedtime routine** If your house is reasonably insulated, you should be able to turn the heating off half an hour before going to bed without noticing any drop in temperature before you crawl under the covers. You should notice a drop in your energy bill, though – of about 5 per cent.

131 **Heat as you go** Unless you've got a good reason to keep your furniture warm, only heat the rooms you're using, regulating each room separately with thermostatic radiator valves.

132 **Unplugged** Electronic appliances can consume almost as much energy during the time they're in standby mode as when they're actively being used – the average TV and video left on standby for a year would use 45kg of CO_2. Switching electronic equipment off properly (at the wall, if necessary) can cut your household electricity bill by up to 10 per cent. This is particularly important for pieces of digital equipment, which often use more energy than analogue equivalents.

133 **Get into hot water** Investigate solar water heating as a source of completely free hot water and central heating to your home. Installation costs are falling, and there may be grants available to help you offset the expense.

134 **Be a jean genie** More than 300g of fertilizers and pesticides are used to produce the average pair of jeans. Don't let this happen on your account: buy a pair made from organic cotton. Alternatively, customize a second-hand pair to suit your style. The only resources needed are a skilled pair of eyes in a charity shop!

135 Timeless style Ask yourself whether you'll like your exciting new interiors scheme in a year or two. Classic, stylish home decoration needs renewing only when it gets tatty, whereas the latest magazine look will quickly appear outdated.

136 The gift of vision When your lens prescription needs renewing or you want to change your frame style, ask your optician if they are one of the many that collect spectacles for reuse in developing countries. If they're not, ask them to join this scheme.

137 Slimmer chiller If you need to buy a new fridge, consider scaling down to a smaller model. Although meat, fish and dairy products need to be refrigerated, many of the other things we put in the fridge would keep just as well in a naturally cool cupboard or larder (with an airbrick installed in a wall if you live in a temperate climate).

138 **CUT YOUR CLOTH** Minimize the need for cooling or heating in your workplace by persuading your employer to relax its dress code during very hot or cold weather. Take your lead from the Japanese government, which runs a publicity campaign encouraging business people to wear short sleeves in the summer to cut down on air conditioning in their offices.

---

139 **Forward-thinking DIY** Have you thought about how you'll get that bedframe you've just assembled back down the stairs when you move house? Use screws instead of nails or glue so that pieces of flatpack furniture can be dismantled easily and reused in their original or another form in the future.

140 **Natural immunity** Our immune systems can cope with – and actually need – exposure to normal household germs. Waging chemical warfare on these organisms alters our homes' microbial balance, encouraging resilient bacteria that can become super-resistant – even to antibiotics. Harsh chemical disinfectants can also affect our central nervous system and organs, and disrupt hormone function. Instead, try natural disinfectants such as tea tree oil, borax and citrus oils.

141 **Keep a green journal** In a notebook or diary (made from recycled paper, of course!), record each time you and your family take a planet-saving action. You could also write about your feelings – the highs and the lows – as you make progress, or perhaps encounter obstacles.

Your green journal would be a good place to **monitor your utility bills (142)**. Record the number of units of energy or water your household consumes during each billing period. When you've been going for more than a year, you'll be able to compare like with like: winter with winter, summer with summer. Little by little, your journal will enable you to keep track – practically, emotionally and financially – of your journey toward a greener life.

143 **Occupational hazards** As if the prospect of falling off a ladder weren't bad enough, decorators have a 40 per cent increased risk of lung cancer because of their exposure to the volatile organic compounds (VOCs) and solvents found in many paints. So try to use natural paints made from plant and mineral bases or ones with low VOC ratings to avoid the health and environmental problems associated with emissions from solvent-based paints.

144 **Boys' toys** Do you really need or want a complete selection of power tools? Unless you're the most avid DIY fan, you'll probably use them only once or twice a year. So why not rent professional-grade ones from a hire shop on the rare occasions that you do need them, or **club together with neighbours to buy a communal set (145)**? That way less energy and fewer resources are used to get your jobs done, and you benefit from better products (and more storage space!).

146   **Clean without chlorine** Many detergents and other cleaning products contain chlorine, which when mixed with other compounds can produce toxic gases. Each chlorine atom can destroy tens of thousands of ozone molecules – bad news, given that chlorine concentrations in the upper atmosphere have quadrupled in the last 25 years. So look for chlorine-free detergents, toilet cleaners, disinfectants and bleach.

147   **Day to remember** As an alternative to another unneeded or unwanted piece of kit, give someone you love a gift that takes up space only in the memory, such as a beauty treatment, concert ticket or trip to a favourite restaurant.

148   **Automate your outgoings** Paying bills will never be entirely painless, but you can eliminate much of the hassle and environmental impact by registering to receive and settle them online. Not only does this save time and cut down on trips to the postbox, it also reduces paper waste and pollution associated with mail transport, and trims your postage costs. You can even schedule automatic bill payments so you'll never miss a payment or pay a late fee again!

149 **RE-DEPLOY YOUR SPARE PAINT** Making paint is an energy-hungry process that produces more than 10 tonnes of waste for every tonne of paint. So make the most of it: rather than letting leftover paint languish in the basement until it's too dried out to use, ask a local school, health centre or community project whether they'd like a fresh lick of paint. There may even be a community paint collection in your area.

150 **Read the small print** Many of the unguents we anoint ourselves with to mask our blemishes are hiding more than a few imperfections of their own. It's worth reading the label and looking into the properties and health and environmental impacts of complicated-sounding ingredients (see page 370). Avoid the worst culprits whenever you can. For example, **steer clear of parabens (151)**, such as methylparaben, ethylparaben and propylparaben, which are used as preservatives in cosmetics and toiletries. These chemicals act as "endocrine disruptors", which means that they can mimic, interfere with or block hormones in humans and animals, and may be linked to breast cancer.

152 **Enjoy the sweet smell of manure** This can of course be taken literally by real enthusiasts, but the rest of us can seek out soap and candles scented with vanilla essence ingeniously extracted from cow dung by Japanese scientists.

153 **Stargazing** Spend a night camping out under the stars with just a groundsheet as basic ground cover to reconnect with the Earth around you and the universe beyond.

154 **Risk-free lacquer** If you want to keep your fingers and toes well dressed, use a water-based nail polish. Unlike solvent-based slicks, these don't contain formaldehyde or phthalates, which can damage both your health and the environment. Water-based versions come in beautiful colours and dry to the touch in just three minutes.

155 **Magic pan** It takes the same amount of time – and energy – to cook a stir-fry as it does to reheat the typical ready meal, and that's not including the energy used to create the ready meal in the first place. The stir-fry will almost certainly taste much nicer and be better for you!

156 **Bamboo bathrobe** Bizarre though it sounds, tough bamboo fibre makes luxuriously soft towels. Bamboo is three times more absorbent than cotton and boasts anti-bacterial, anti-static and anti-fungal properties. It grows quickly, and without any need for pesticides, which makes it a fantastically eco-friendly material. Ask any panda!

157 **Put your feet up** Minimize the need to clean your floors by placing doormats inside and outside external doors and asking people to take their shoes off as they come in. Who said that saving the planet was hard work?

158 **Squash your rubbish** Minimize the impact of the rubbish you can't avoid producing by squashing it before you bin it. This way it will take up less space in landfill sites or recycling depots – and pummelling it is a great stress-buster as well!

159 **Keep your thermostat cosy** To avoid overheating your home, make sure that the thermostat connected to your boiler is on an internal wall in one of the main living areas in your home, rather than, say, your chilly utility room.

160 **Wasteful art** If you enjoy making art, next time you need to stock up on materials don't go to the art shop, but take a look in your dustbin. With a little imagination, you can transform waste products into striking artworks. **Take inspiration from the Soweto Mountain of Hope (Somoho) project (161)** in South Africa, which has turned a growing waste problem into an internationally celebrated community art resource.

162 **TALK TO STRANGERS** Many of us, particularly die-hard urbanites, find the idea of talking to strangers intimidating – we may not even know our neighbours very well. But conversations with people you don't normally talk to can lead in all kinds of directions – the final destination could well be a happier, friendlier world for both you and them.

163 **Egg your plants on** Water that has had eggs boiled in it is enriched with calcium. Pouring it on your garden, once it's cooled, rather than down the sink, will save a little water and feed your plants.

164 **Quick-hit stain removal** Here are just a few ways to remove troublesome stains without resorting to environmentally unfriendly cleaning methods. Rub white chalk into oil stains before washing; remove tea, coffee, chocolate and blood with one part borax to eight parts water; tackle grass stains with glycerine (available from chemists); and bleach white clothes by laying them out in the sun.

165 **Buff up your polishing** Avoid commercial furniture polishes, which tend to be made from flammable petroleum distillates (linked with lung and skin cancer) and toxic nitrobenzene. Instead, try natural products based on beeswax or olive oil, or you can even **make your own polish (166)** using three parts olive oil to one part vinegar.

167 **The true meaning of dry cleaning** The solvents used in dry-cleaning processes are toxic to humans (especially the unfortunate dry-cleaning staff) and the environment. The simplest way to avoid contributing to this damage is to choose clothes that don't need dry cleaning. You can also **keep clothes fresh for longer between cleans (168)** by airing and brushing them, if appropriate, after each wearing. Some "dry clean only" garments can actually be washed conventionally: **carefully try washing silks and woollens by hand in cold water (169)**. If you feel nervous about this, it's probably best to start with something other than your most treasured silk scarf or tie until you've seen for yourself that it works. Another alternative is to **seek out "wet cleaning" or "green" dry-cleaning services (170)**, which use liquid carbon dioxide or silicon-based solvents in place of harmful substances.

171 **A cooler wash** Clothes very rarely need to be washed at high temperatures. By washing at 40 degrees instead of 60, your washing machine will use 30 per cent less energy, and your clothes will last longer.

172 **Say no to junk mail** Protect your home and office from a relentless avalanche of wasteful junk mail by registering with a mail preference service (see page 373). To drive the message home, **place a "no junk mail" sticker on your letterbox (173)**. You may be able to get one from your local authority's waste-management department or you can make your own.

174   **Go on a staple diet** This might seem like a tiny action, but if all of the USA's 75 million white-collar workers used one fewer staple each day, they'd make a daily saving of 2,500kg of steel – that's 900 tonnes a year. Scale down your staple habit, and use paper clips instead, which have the advantage of being reusable.

175   **Cheers!** Many off-licences will lend proper glasses free of charge if you buy drinks from them. Use these for your next party and cut back on party waste.

176 **TREE OF LIFE** Mark significant events in your life by planting a tree: it will absorb CO_2 and other forms of pollution, provide a home to hundreds of creatures, help create and retain soil, and perform many other valuable ecological functions. It will also be a thing of beauty, and a lasting legacy of your time on Earth. If you don't have access to land on which to plant a tree, a number of organizations will plant one on your behalf.

---

177 **Drip-dry your hands** It's hard to calculate whether it's more environmentally damaging to dry your hands with an electric dryer (generally powered from non-renewable resources) or paper towels, which contain wood and other valuable resources. Save yourself this headache by doing neither: give your hands a quick shake (or wipe them on your trousers). Just use a natural hand cream from time to time if you're worried about chapping.

178 **Deter fleas naturally** To keep biting pests away from your furry friends, try smuggling a clove of finely chopped or crushed garlic into your pets' food twice a week. This makes their blood unappetizing to parasites, and so avoids the need for conventional flea powders, collars and sprays, which contain toxic organophosphates and pesticides associated with animal, human and environmental health problems. Reinforce this line of defence (and counteract any smell from the garlic) by **putting rosemary and lavender in your pets' beds (179)** or neem or citrus oil on their coats.

180 **Declare war on packaging** Supposedly designed to make our lives easier, the multi-layered packaging that envelops many mainstream grocery products can often be more of a hindrance than a help – and, of course, the effect on the environment is wholly negative. Fortunately, there are numerous ways in which you can help turn the tide. **Buy non-perishable items in bulk packages (181)** or buy food loose and then store it in your own minimal, reusable packaging. **Look for products sold in refillable containers (182)** and make the effort to reuse them. Write to the manufacturers of your favourite brands to ask them to provide this kind of packaging if they don't already. Similarly, **point out the madness (183)**: if you see a blatantly overpackaged product (cellophane-wrapped coconuts, anyone?), let stockists and suppliers know how you feel. It's likely they'll look again at how their wares are perceived – it's not in their commercial interests to lose their customers' good will.

As a last resort, **unwrap excessively packaged purchases in the shop (184)** and ask the staff to deal with the waste. That packaging gets added to the cost of our shopping (supermarket shoppers unwittingly spend a sixth or more of their food budget on packaging), so you've got a right to be annoyed!

185   **Dispose of disposables** Most disposable items add little to our quality of life but a lot to waste mountains. Try to use them only in emergencies, and go for less wasteful alternatives. For example, **cover food with a dish, plate or lid (186)** instead of aluminium foil or cling film, and **wipe up spillages with tea towels and dish cloths (187)** instead of kitchen paper. If you're a fan of barbecues and picnics, **buy some unbreakable cutlery and crockery (188)** to use in place of flimsy disposable plastic items.

189 **TWO SIDES TO EVERY STORY** Whether printing a long formal report at work or doodling while you chat on the phone, try to use both sides of the paper. You'll get through half the volume of wood and other resources used to make it, and cut CO_2 emissions by 2.5kg for every kilo of paper you save. **If your printer has a duplex (double-sided) function, make it a default option (190)** – that way you have to make an adjustment only on the few occasions when single-sided printing is essential.

---

191 **Robust rust remover** To clean metal affected by rust or calcium deposits, use white vinegar, aided with a wire brush if necessary.

192 **Season's greetings** To cut down on the amount of extra paper being whizzed around the globe at Christmas, send electronic greetings by e-mail. A number of environmental charities offer e-cards via their websites.

For friends who don't have an e-mail address, **buy paper cards directly from a charity (193)**. The good cause is likely to receive more of the proceeds than if you buy charity cards from a mainstream outlet, and they're usually made from recycled card (particularly those from environmental charities). **Recycle cards you receive (194)**, either through a local authority scheme to raise money for charity, or by turning them into gift tags for next Christmas.

195 **Collected works** Most people don't like racing around endlessly on errands. But in our haste to get chores ticked off immediately, we often fall into this trap. Save time, energy and transport costs by looking for ways to pool all your errands into one or two extended circuits each week.

196 **Keep it simple** Shun products packaged in mixed materials, such as plastic and foil, as they're complicated and expensive to recycle. If you do find such an item in your cupboards, **try to dismantle it into its constituent materials (197)** before putting it out for recycling.

198 **Longevity** When you're buying equipment for your home or office, make sure it will last. Check that it can be easily repaired and that the manufacturer will supply spare parts. It's also worth investing a little more in products that have a long guarantee.

199 **Getting antsy about ants?** To drive ants out of your home without resorting to extermination, work out how they're getting in and block the hole, or make the entrance unattractive from an ant's perspective with a squeeze of lemon juice. They also hate talcum powder, chalk, bone meal, charcoal dust and cayenne pepper, so try making barriers using any of these to persuade them to go elsewhere.

200   **Look before you leap** To avoid wasting paper on typos and other blunders, have a really good look at your document on screen before you hit the print button. Run spellcheck and look at the print preview to make sure that your work is formatted to your satisfaction.

201   **Build a green house** If you're embarking on any kind of building project, you're much more likely to get the eco-friendly results you want if your architect has green credentials (see page 372). Look for one who's up to date on the latest green materials, techniques and technologies, and the experience should be a pleasant adventure. If they roll their eyes at the first mention of a low-energy lightbulb, you may have a battle on your hands.

202   **As good as new** Donate your worn-out sofa, chairs or table to local furniture recyclers. They'll turn your unwanted clobber into another piece of covetable kit, saving it from the rubbish heap.

203 **Grounded holidays** Travelling by land or sea gives you the chance to really take in your surroundings, to have some adventures along the way and often to arrive almost as quickly as you would by plane (and better rested). Plan a flight-free holiday (see page 373) and not only will you avoid check-in queues, but your trip won't produce anywhere near as much pollution: trains produce 20 times less emissions per passenger mile than planes, and ships almost 200 times less.

204 **Load up the kids with recycling** Schools are generally keen to receive materials such as magazines, newspapers, boxes and leftover wallpaper – they'll find good second homes in arts and crafts classes, as table coverings, or even as a liner for the school bunny's hutch!

205 **EVERY LAST SCRAP** Recycle all your paper, not just newspapers and magazines. Every tonne of paper reused leaves 17 trees standing, looking beautiful and working hard to absorb CO_2 on our behalf.

206 **Protect your clothes with zest** Dried lemon peel is a natural moth deterrent – simply sprinkle pieces in your drawers, or tie a few pieces in cheesecloth and hang them in your wardrobe.

207 **Don't be a water importer** Water's undoubtedly good for your health, but when it comes in a plastic bottle and has been transported long distances, not so good for that of the planet. In the developed world we're lucky enough to have safe drinking water piped, packaging-free, into our homes for a tiny fraction of the cost of bottled water, yet sales of bottles continue to rise.

Try the following steps to kick the bottled-water habit. **Keep a jug of tap water in the fridge (208)** – when chilled it's almost indistinguishable from mineral water. If you're worried about water quality, **invest in a filtration system for your kitchen tap (209)**. Good intentions are easily eroded when you're on the hoof – which is also when you tend to be thirstiest. To avoid having to buy endless plastic bottles of water, **pack a small, robust drinking bottle and refill it en route (210)**.

211   **In good odour** Synthetic musks (often called "parfum") crop up in an array of products – from cleaning potions to posh perfumes. They're very persistent compounds that aren't broken down easily, and have been found in places as unlikely as mussels, human body fat, breast milk and fish. They're potential hormone disrupters, and so best avoided. Instead, **choose perfumes based on natural oils (212)** for yourself. And in your home, **make commercial air fresheners redundant (213)** by opening windows, absorbing offending pongs with a bowl of baking soda dissolved in water, boiling some cinnamon, choosing products perfumed with citronella or other natural oils, or squirting a blend of water and lavender oil from a spray bottle.

214   **Winds of change** As well as reducing your energy use, make sure that the energy you do need comes from a carbon-neutral source (see page 21). Switching to one of the growing number of companies supplying energy from renewable sources such as wind, sun and biomass usually only involves a phone call, after which your home electricity use won't contribute to CO_2 emissions.

215 **Industrial revolution** Find out more about the ideas of the American industrial designer William McDonough by reading his book *Cradle to Cradle* (2002). McDonough is rethinking industrial processes to eliminate waste at source, with the ultimate aim that all by-products of manufacturing should be suitable either to feed the soil or to be remade, "upcycled", into something else.

216 Stock your stock pot Water used for cooking vegetables makes great stock for soups and sauces. If you're not planning to cook again soon, you can still use those nutrients and avoid wasting that water by pouring it onto plants rather than down the drain.

217 ODD SOCKS, EVEN TEMPERATURE It's a law of nature that every household contains an extended family of neglected odd socks. Give the biggest ones a second career by stuffing them with old rags, stitching the ends closed and laying them along the bottom of doors to block out chilly draughts.

218 Car clubber Do you really need a car all day every day? If you need to use a car only occasionally, you could share the cost, avoid the hassles and minimize the environmental impact of car ownership by joining a car-share scheme or car club (see page 373). For a monthly fee and/or hourly rate, you can call upon a well-maintained car whenever you need it, and then hand it back. No more Sundays polishing hubcaps!

219   **Dental arithmetic** Turning the tap off while brushing your teeth saves up to 10 litres of water each time. Assuming two brushings a day, that adds up to more than 500,000 litres over the average person's lifetime.

220   **Only the finest ingredients** If you really want to know what you're putting onto your clothes and skin and sending down your drain, make your own washing powder using a cup of grated natural soap, a cup of washing soda and a couple of teaspoons of lavender oil.

221   **Lower your flow** Install low-flow aerating fittings to your shower and taps. These ingenious devices reduce water flow by up to 50 per cent, but because they sprinkle in fine jets or mix air bubbles into the water, you feel like you're getting just as wet.

222   **Use a washing-up bowl** Rather than doing the dishes under a running tap, use a washing-up bowl full of hot, soapy water. Refill the bowl with clean water for rinsing, and you'll still use only a fraction of the water you would if you kept the tap running.

223 **Set a cat curfew** Pet cats can have a huge impact on wildlife. For example, Britain's eight million domestic cats (and one million feral ones) kill up to 300 million wild birds and mammals every year – that's about one every ten days for each cat. You can help reduce the carnage by keeping your moggie indoors during the hour after sunrise and the hour before sunset, which is when birds are most active. As an extra measure, **kit your cat out with a collar fitted with a bell or sonic device (224).** These give prey a chance to escape, cutting kill rates by up to 40 per cent. Make sure the collar has a quick-release mechanism to stop your cat choking if it gets caught on something.

225 **Pedal practice** If you don't feel confident about you or your children cycling on roads, enrol your family in a cycling-proficiency course to build up your skills and road awareness. Your local authority may offer free or subsidized classes.

226 **Rail versus road** How many business documents, novels or love letters can you read (or write) while you're driving? Try taking your next long trip by train rather than car. It will almost always be faster, and you'll be able to enjoy the scenery without endangering anyone's life. You'll also arrive with a much greater sense of achievement (even if only because you've had a decent sleep) than you would if you'd been stuck behind the wheel.

227 **Drought-proof your garden** If you have a dry garden, plant drought-tolerant species, such as agapanthus, echinacea and sedum, which can survive long periods with little or no water (see page 373).

228 **Water wisely** The best times to water the garden are the early morning or the evening. Water evaporates more slowly when it's cool, so more will get to where it's needed and less will be wasted. You'll also avoid the scorching effect of water droplets on your plants' leaves in strong sunlight.

Use a watering can rather than a sprinkler (229): that way you can direct water to the base of each of your plants rather than showering your neighbour's drive. A sprinkler can use up to 650 litres of water an hour – that's a whopping 5,200 litres if you leave it on overnight. **If you use a hosepipe, fit a trigger nozzle (230)**, so you can shut off the flow when carrying the hose from one plant to the next.

231 **Easy does it** Wait until the washing machine's full before you do a wash. Each washing machine cycle uses more than 100 litres of water, so make sure you're getting the most from every drop.

232 **Comfort blanket** Mulch around your plants each spring when the ground is moist to help stop water evaporating from the soil's surface and instead get it down to the roots. A layer, at least 7cm thick, of bark chips, straw, grass clippings or organic compost will keep water in, stop sunlight stimulating weed growth and add nutrients to the soil.

233 **No jacket required** Install a "tankless" water heater or combination boiler to save as much as 50 per cent of the cost of heating your water. These space-saving, highly energy-efficient heaters burn energy only when you need hot water. This eliminates standby heat loss which can be as high as 3–4 per cent every hour for water heaters linked to a storage tank.

234 **Can you use your water twice?** "Grey" water – water that's been used in sinks, baths, showers or the washing machine – can be used again to flush toilets, or to water the garden if it contains only biodegradable soaps. Some new houses incorporate grey-water recycling systems, and they can also be retrofitted.

235   **Bath or shower?** The average bath uses about 80 litres of water, while the average shower uses about half that. Save water by reserving baths for special occasions.

Of course, showers use less water than baths only if you don't stand under them for too long. **Try to keep your showering time below five minutes (236)**, or you'll be using at least as much water as you would in a bath. An egg-timer suction-cupped onto the shower wall is a good way of keeping track, and makes showering a fun race against time for kids. And **avoid high-pressure power showers (237)**, which guzzle water.

238   **Pleasant valet Sunday** Next time you reach for the chamois leather, ask yourself whether your car really needs a wash. You might not want your mean machine to suffer the indignity of having "clean me" finger-traced into its grime, but the ritual car cleansing every Sunday morning may be taking things too far the other way.

Besides washing your car less often, try using less water each time. If you **wash your car with a bucket and sponge (239)**, you'll generally use about 10 litres of water, whereas using a hose will get you through around 100 litres. Like your garden, **your car will benefit from being tended to with rainwater (240)** from a water butt, which is often softer than tap water and so breaks down dirt and grease more effectively.

If you're not a fan of washing your car yourself, don't despair. Just make sure you **go to a carwash that has installed a water-recycling system (241)**. These can reuse 95 per cent of the water from each wash.

242   **Do your plants really need purified drinking water?**
Rather than treating your plants to highly processed drinking-quality water from the tap, consider connecting a water butt to the downpipe from your roof to collect rainwater, which is actually much better for them.

243   **On flushing** Up to a third of the drinking water that comes into the average Western home goes straight down the toilet, which is a crazy waste of this precious (and highly processed) resource. To reduce the volume per flush, **try putting a plastic bottle filled with water into the cistern (244)**. If you're installing a new bathroom, **specify a dual-flush toilet (245)**, which allows you to choose flush volume according to "load". Finally, and more controversially, **ask yourself whether you really need to flush (246)** every time you use the toilet. Without going into details, just make sure you leave the lid down if you decide not to flush!

247 **Never flush a nappy** Putting a disposable nappy down the toilet unleashes a string of horrors. The absorbent gel they contain is so effective that they can swell enough to block even the broadest of pipes, and meanwhile their bleaching agent seeps into waterways, where it can damage plants, wildlife and people. Any nappies that make it through the processing system wash up on riverbanks and beaches. So, if you must use them, put them in the bin!

248 **And another thing** Not only do disposable nappies harm the environment, but there's also evidence that their plastic linings can increase the temperature of baby boys' scrotums by up to 1 per cent, which has been associated with a drop in adult male fertility levels.

249 **PACK YOUR OWN LUNCH** Get yourself a few sturdy containers of different sizes, an unbreakable bottle and/or flask, buy some bulk supplies at the beginning of each week, and let your imagination run wild. With the cash you'll save by not buying heavily packaged convenience foods or eating out, you can afford a different treat every day.

---

250 **Bed baby down naturally** When choosing cot bedding, go for natural fabrics such as cotton, wool, silk or hemp. These breathable materials help to regulate your baby's body temperature. Choose fabrics that are labelled organic to be sure you're avoiding the chemical pesticide and fertilizer residues present on even "natural" fabrics, which can be absorbed through babies' delicate skin.

251 **Nappies without tears** Use eco-friendly nappy soak to presoak reusable nappies before washing them using eco-balls (see page 264) for an all-round low-impact baby's bottom.

252 **Spend a day without spending** Every now and then, try
to manage without consuming anything bought with money.
You may be surprised how easy (and enjoyable!) it is to get
by on things you've grown, made or simply had in your
home for ages. If you like to feel part of a movement,
join International Buy Nothing Day on the fourth

Thursday of November in Canada and the USA, and on the
following Saturday in the rest of the world. Leave your wallet
at home and see what happens.

253   **Buy some hemp paper** Paper made from hemp uses only
a quarter of the land required to produce paper from timber,
and the paper is of a much higher quality.

254   **A click a day** Around 24,000 people die from hunger every
day. Visit www.thehungersite.com, click the "give free food"
button, and the website's sponsors donate the equivalent of
a cup of food to a hungry person on your behalf. If you set
it up as your home page, you can give a cup every
time you go online.

255   **Bad business** Think twice before you buy wildlife
products, as they could threaten endangered species
and even be illegal. Avoid jewellery and other items made from
sea turtle shells, elephant ivory or coral, and if you buy plants
such as orchids, cacti and cycads, make sure they haven't been
collected from the wild.

256 **BE A GREEN BOOKWORM** Make sure your thirst for knowledge has a minimal environmental impact by choosing books that are printed on paper that's recycled or from guaranteed sustainable sources (like this one!). If the book you're after isn't available in this form, borrow it from the library instead, and let the publishers know why they've missed out on a sale.

257 **Wise up** Environmental issues and innovations are developing at quite a pace. To keep up to date, take out a subscription to a specialist magazine or journal, such as *The Ecologist*. This particular title is available in many different countries, as well as online. If you receive a printed copy, don't forget to circulate it among friends and colleagues or donate it to your local doctor's surgery or hairdresser's salon once you've read it.

258 **Cruising along** On long, open stretches of road, cruise control can save fuel by helping your car maintain a steady speed.

259 **Home and dry** While in action, tumble dryers consume more energy than any other household appliance, so if you have one, try to use it only as a last resort, and hang clothes out to dry instead (outside, if possible, to make them smell really fresh). Cutting your tumble-dryer use by just one load a week will reduce your home's CO_2 emissions by around 90kg a year. If you have to use the tumble dryer, **keep the filter lint-free (260)** and **run loads back to back while the drum's still hot (261).**

262   **Headscratcher** Headlice are a common irritation of childhood. But the side effects of chemical lice treatments are potentially a lot worse than irritating – they can include hyperactivity, rashes and disruption of the immune system. To achieve insect-free tresses the natural way, coat your child's hair in natural hair conditioner, comb through with a wide-tooth comb and repeat from root to tip with a fine-toothed nit comb to remove the lice. You need to repeat this treatment every couple of days for a week to remove any larvae that may have hatched in the meantime.

263   **Have you got a leaky home?** If you have a water meter, you can detect hidden water leaks by reading it at the beginning and end of a two-hour period when no water is being used. If the two readings are different, there's a leak. Track it down and fix it!

264 **Turn on, tune in, log out** Give someone (perhaps yourself) an MP3 player and a voucher for some internet downloads. Once they've worked out how to track down their favourite music online, they need never buy another CD. **Throw in a solar-powered or clockwork MP3 charger (265)** and their musical enjoyment can be carbon-neutral from now on.

266 **A priceless gift** In our hectic modern lifestyles, time is often what we value most. If you don't see as much of a good friend as you'd like, rather than buying them a hastily chosen gift, arrange to spend some time with them. It doesn't really matter what you choose to do – it's the opportunity to catch up that's important. And then if you do want to buy them a gift another time, you'll have a better idea what they might like.

267 **Flex your consumer muscles** If you don't like the way certain companies operate – whether the materials or processes they use or the pollution they produce – tell them! Every business ultimately depends on you to buy their products or services, and the impacts of consumer action are huge. If organized campaigns aren't your thing, simply **switch your**

shopping habits (268) – purchasing power really counts. But you'll have even more impact if you write a polite letter to the company explaining why you're not spending money with them.

269 **Natural mobile** Inspire your baby with a hand-made mobile over his or her cot. Instil early memories of natural objects such as driftwood, shells, leaves and feathers lovingly collected and tied onto a wooden frame.

270 **That's a wrap** Use recycled wrapping paper to wrap gifts for your loved ones. Buy giftwrap and tags made from recycled paper, and use ribbons or string rather than sticky tape so the paper can be folded up and used again.

271 **Ten thousand steps** Health experts recommend that we walk 10,000 steps a day (roughly equivalent to 5 miles) to maintain good health. So get yourself a pedometer and give yourself a small reward each time you exceed this target. Knowing you're keeping your body healthy makes the decision not to drive to the shops much easier.

272 **SOAK UP IDEAS** Discover more about other cultures, religions, mindsets and ways of life. It's likely that other people are already tackling some of the things you'd like to see changed. Join in. Share ideas. Look and learn.

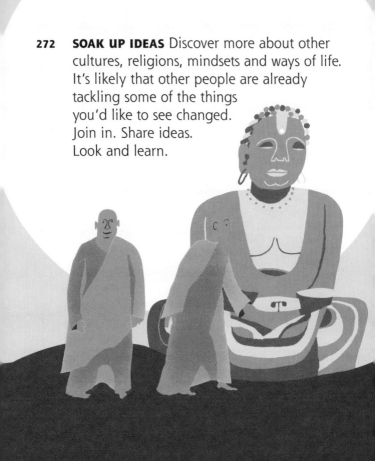

273 **Keep chemical waste out of waterways** Never pour paints, used oil, cleaning solvents, polishes, pool chemicals, insecticides, and other hazardous household chemicals down drains, sinks or toilets. Many of these products contain harmful substances such as petroleum distillates, sodium hypochlorite, ammonia and formaldehyde which could end up in nearby water bodies if not disposed of properly. Contact your local sanitation, public works or environmental health department to find out about hazardous waste collection days and sites. If a local programme isn't available, ask for one.

274 **Snap-happy** Taking pictures with a digital camera means you can weed out the blurred shots of your thumb before you waste cash and resources printing them out. However, if you prefer to use a film camera, **choose 36- instead of 24-exposure films (275)** to reduce the price, packaging and processing chemicals by a third per snap.

276 **Keep the pressure off** Whether or not you have low flow fittings on your taps and shower, make sure you turn them on only far enough to provide the water you need. Let's face it, you don't need a particularly powerful jet of water to wash your hands or wet a toothbrush.

277 **Help stamp out animal cruelty** If you suspect that an animal is being mistreated – either at home or abroad – report the incident to the Born Free Foundation. Their "travellers' alert" online campaign (see page 373) seeks to bring to justice the perpetrators of animal cruelty and neglect.

278 **Protective sanitary products** The average woman uses 10,000 sanitary products during her lifetime. These tend to be treated with chlorine bleaches, and the dioxins produced are damaging to the environment and to our bodies. **Choose tampons and towels that haven't been bleached with chlorine (279)** and that are made from organic cotton, if possible.

To avoid the need for the vast majority of those 10,000 sanitary products, **try wearing a menstrual cup (280)**. This hygienic bell-shaped silicon container works without leakage or discomfort. It can be washed and reused thousands of times, saving tonnes of unnecessary waste and a pile of money.

281 **Chock-a-block** Keep your freezer as full as possible: it takes more energy to chill empty space. If you don't need to stock up on food at the moment, empty cardboard boxes will achieve the same result.

282 **Bright lights** Make sure you're getting the full benefit of the energy going into your lights by wiping dust off lighting fixtures and bulbs every few months (make sure that the bulbs are cool first).

283 **A world of toys** Make some toys for your children or help them to come up with their own. Beanbags made from fabric from an old T-shirt stuffed with (uncooked!) lentils, rag dolls made from dresses or shirts, or a dressing-up box filled with hand-me-downs or jumble-sale finds will provide months of fun at little cost.

284 **Take in a lodger** If you've got a spare room in your home, consider renting it out. Inhabitants of a shared home each use fewer resources than they would if they lived on their own. They also generally save money – and are less likely to suffer from loneliness!

285 **Cherish your milkman** If you've got a milk-delivery service in your area, use it. It will generally provide milk from local herds, and take back milk bottles for washing and reuse – an even better option than recycling.

286 **School trip** Offer to help organize a field trip or nature walk for your child's class at school. Experiencing nature first hand will help to bring any future lessons about the environment to life.

287 NEW LEASE OF LIFE Just because you no longer want something doesn't mean it's junk – and it could even make you some money. Try selling unwanted items online (try eBay), donating them to a new home (try Freecycle; see page 273) or swapping them with neighbours via a community swap shop. These could also be sources of replacement items for yourself.

288 **Dry your dishes naturally** Save energy by switching off your dishwasher before the drying cycle. Open the dishwasher after the final rinse, and the hot dishes will dry quickly on their own.

---

289 **A SENSE OF WONDER** Appreciating nature's diversity can be the first step in developing a caring relationship with our incredible planet. So take your children on a bug foray, stream survey or birdwatching outing, and try to learn about a few new creatures each time. For an exhilarating overview of the landscape, take your kids on a trip in a hot-air balloon.

---

290 **Minimal lighting** Make sure that any outdoor lights around your home point downward so they shine light only where it's really needed. Replace halogen lights with low-power compact fluorescent bulbs and switch them on only when they're required.

291 **Put your kettle on the back burner** Fill a Thermos® flask with water left over when you boil the kettle, and use that for your next few hot drinks rather than boiling the kettle every time.

292   **Keep them guessing** Strengthen your vegetable garden's resistance to pests by rotating your crops each year. This will help stop pests who are passionate about a particular plant building up in the soil and surrounding habitats.

293   **Hidden charge** If you leave your mobile phone charger plugged in all the time, up to 95 per cent of the energy it consumes will go to waste. You can tell when the charger is using electricity because it feels warm. So, always unplug your charger when it's not in use, and **don't leave your phone to charge overnight (294)** – it only takes a couple of hours to get revved up.

Alternatively, **invest in a wind-up phone charger (295)**, which you can use absolutely anywhere. It takes three minutes of charging to power an eight-minute chat, which means keen conversationalists will get very toned forearms!

296   **Pressed for time** When ironing, leave garments that require a cool iron until last. You should be able to turn the iron off and press them flat with the residual heat if you work quickly enough!

297   **Shutdown routine** Before you leave your desk at the end of the day, take a moment to check that everything's switched off. Leaving your computer on overnight can waste enough energy to laser-print 800 A4 pages. That adds up to 2,600kWh of energy each year, producing up to 1.9 tonnes of CO_2, without getting any extra work done!

298   **Grow your own** If you don't have land of your own, find out whether there's a plot available in your local allotment garden. With a few hours' attention each week, this little patch of land could change the way your family eats, get you super fit and wean you off supermarket vegetable aisles for life.

299   **A breath of fresh air** Clear kitchen air naturally by opening the window rather than using an extractor fan, which is often ineffective and noisy – and always a waste of energy.

300   **Don't hide your radiators** In order to do their work properly, radiators and other heaters need to have space to radiate their heat, so don't tuck them behind sofas or curtains.

301   **Home economics** Next time you need to buy a cooker, look for one that will help you save energy (and money). **Choose a gas model (302)**, if possible, as gas is a more direct form of energy usage than electricity and its operating costs should be half those of a similar electric model. If you don't have a gas supply in your area or space for bottled gas, **find an electric cooker with halogen and induction elements (303)** on the hob, which are more efficient than solid disks and radiant elements, and that has a fan oven, which should cut cooking times by up to a third.

However it's powered, **make sure the oven has a glass door and a light (304)** so you can check on your food's progress without needing to open the door and let heat escape.

305   **Pure wool** Although wool is a natural product, the process of producing it is unfortunately not as environmentally friendly as the image of a field of fluffy sheep might suggest. Chemicals such as organophosphates used in sheep dip are toxic and potentially carcinogenic, and can leach into water supplies – as can the chlorine used to make wool shrink-resistant. So seek out products made from wool produced using organic methods, which avoid such compounds.

306 **Salad days** Turn your back on bagged salad leaves. The "modified atmosphere" packaging designed to preserve the leaves and the chlorine used to wash them combine to destroy valuable antioxidant nutrients, and this intensive processing wastes energy. Instead, **buy a whole lettuce (307)** – it'll be much fresher and you'll save enough cash to buy ingredients for a dressing.

Better still, **grow your own salad leaves (308)**. You'll get a decent yield even from a window box. It takes no time and if you sow in batches every two or three weeks, you'll be making delicious salads for months.

309 **Boxing clever** If you don't live near a farmers' market, joining a box scheme is a wonderfully easy way of buying fresh organic produce, and is cheaper than buying organic food from shops. You can specify the precise contents of your weekly delivery or ask for a mixed box of whatever happens to be in season – which can be an exciting introduction to unfamiliar types of fruit and vegetables!

To take things further, **consider joining a CSA (Community Supported Agriculture) scheme (310)**. In return for an annual subscription to a local farm, you'll not only receive a weekly delivery of seasonal produce, but will also often be able to participate in the running of the farm and become part of a lively social network of stakeholders.

311 **Wear a hemp shirt** Hemp has been unfairly saddled with a hair-shirt image, which it doesn't deserve. It's a very ecologically friendly crop, which doesn't need pesticides and herbicides to thrive and is now used to make a wide range of fashionable clothes, as well as other products ranging from frisbees to bags.

312 **Stare at a flat screen** Not only do flat LCD (liquid crystal display) screens mean that your TV and computer monitor take up less space (and look snazzier) than the old-fashioned cathode-ray models, they're also much more efficient, using about 30 per cent less energy. And because they give off less heat and fewer electronic emissions, your living room or office should be healthier and more comfortable. Just make sure that if you're upgrading, you recycle your old kit.

313   **Transparent logic** Glass bottles are among the easiest items to recycle. Doing this not only saves resources (1.2 tonnes of sand, ash and limestone and 135 litres of oil for every tonne of glass recycled), but also cuts energy use – recycling just one bottle saves enough energy to power a television for 90 minutes.

314 **Give shatoosh shawls the cold shoulder** A fabric of desire for some fashionistas, shatoosh wool is plucked from endangered Tibetan antelopes, which are killed for the purpose. If you covet a super-soft shawl, opt for one made from pashmina wool, which is shaved, leaving the animal intact (if a little chilly).

315 **Put your money where your mouth is** Beware: not all bank accounts are equal. While some banks' investment portfolios might include, for example, the arms industry and tobacco firms and give indirect support to oppressive regimes, others avoid such investments and favour companies with good environmental and humanitarian records. So switch your account to an ethical bank, and let your previous one know why you chose to move on.

316 **Distance no object** If you're tying the knot, first of all, congratulations! Second, ask your guests to let you know how far they'll have to travel to reach the ceremony and what method of transport they'll be using, and invest in an offsetting scheme (see page 373) to neutralize the carbon emissions generated.

317   **Lay off the peat** Peat bogs are an ancient and irreplaceable natural habitat, home to a whole host of unique flora and fauna. Unfortunately, they're under threat from human consumption – both for fuel and, primarily, as a base for compost. The best alternative is to produce your own compost, but if you can't make enough for your needs, ask your garden centre to stock one of the growing number of brands of peat-free compost.

318   **Takeaway storage** Plastic takeaway containers can be handy boxes for packed lunches or for storing food. Make sure you wash them thoroughly to get rid of any residual spicy odours. However, if you're a takeaway fan, you'll soon gather more containers than you can usefully use at home. So **take empty containers back (319)** when you order your next meal, and ask for your food to be served in them rather than new boxes. If eyebrows are raised, remind the restaurant that they'll be saving money!

320   **Garden detox** If you've decided to stop using chemical pesticides in your garden, don't chuck the potions still lurking in your shed into the bin or down the drain. They could make their way into drinking-water supplies through either route, poisoning ecosystems along the way. Instead, take these substances to your local recycling centre for safe disposal. Then switch to organic alternatives to avoid the same problems occurring in the future.

321 **Water power** Many large-scale hydroelectric developments, involving the damming of wide valleys, have caused high-profile environmental and social problems, as ecosystems are disrupted and communities displaced. But many countries, from Austria to Nepal, are shifting their focus to smaller-scale hydroelectric projects, which, if responsibly implemented, have relatively small social and environmental impacts, while providing people with power and related economic benefits.

322 **Preservation order** Choose boron- or natural asphalt-based wood preservatives, which penetrate wood without using harmful solvents. The conventional alternatives contain highly toxic nerve poisons and fungicides, and continue to damage the environment for a long time after they've been applied.

323 **Refreshing thought** Use a glass at the water cooler instead of disposable plastic cups or paper cones.

324 **Grow a spud tower** For a bumper harvest from a small space, plant some seed potatoes under a couple of inches of compost inside an old tyre. When the plants are about 20cm tall, put another tyre on top and fill with more compost so that only 5cm of the growth is left above the surface. You can repeat this process until your tower is four or five tyres tall. When buried, the stem becomes root, which sends off potato-producing lateral roots, multiplying the yield from each seed potato.

325 **Join a green gym** Working out on energy-hungry exercise machines in an air-conditioned, windowless box while watching soap operas or rock videos is a strange and often unenjoyable feature of modern life. To get fit in more natural surroundings, look for a "green gym" in your area. These groups organize environmental projects, such as tree planting, hedge laying and developing school nature areas and public green spaces, which provide the health-giving effects of outdoor exercise while benefiting your community. You can burn up to 30 per cent more calories an hour building a footpath than doing aerobics, and you'll learn a lot more skills!

326   **BUY LOCAL AND SEASONAL** Do you need to get your apples from New Zealand and your asparagus from Peru? Resist the supermarket "all-year-round" mentality and get back in tune with local, seasonal produce. You'll reduce the amount of air freight emissions associated with your meal, and support your local farmers.

327 **Ethical aquarium** A fish tank can be a soothing mini-ecosystem in your home or office. But make sure it's not threatening marine populations: stock it with fish that are certified by the Marine Aquarium Council as unendangered species. And **don't buy coral to adorn your tank (328)**, as it's in serious decline in many areas.

329 **Wwoof your way around the world** If you hanker for a change from the beach, why not spend time working on an organic farm during your next holiday? The international WWOOF (World-Wide Opportunities on Organic Farms) association can put you in touch with host farms. This is a great way to encounter places, people and adventures that are not available to the average tourist.

330 **Woolly lining** If you've had a moth attack in your wardrobe, try using any unsalvageable woolly jumpers or blankets to line a couple of hanging baskets to cheer up your garden in the spring.

331 **Security measure** If you leave a light on when you go away, set it on a timer and make sure you use an energy-efficient bulb.

332 **Organic holiday** Enjoy the benefits of organic produce in beautiful surroundings by staying at one of a growing international network of hotels, guesthouses and farms that specialize in organic hospitality (see page 372).

333 **Green globe** When planning your holiday, try to book with members of Green Globe 21 – a worldwide certification programme dedicated to helping the travel and tourism industry develop in sustainable ways.

334 **Don't be a water hog on holiday** Water supplies are a particularly acute concern in hot climates. It's easy to squander resources when you're pampering yourself – the average holidaymaker in Spain, for example, uses twice as much water as each resident. Minimize the impact of your visit by not insisting on a clean towel every day, not bathing more than you would at home, and generally using water carefully.

335 **Dinner time!** Cook a meal from scratch: buy all the ingredients from local suppliers if you can, and invite your family and friends to help with the cooking – and, of course, the eating.

336   **Smokin'** Firing up the barbecue is a great way to enjoy time outdoors. But make sure the only environmental nuisance caused by your alfresco dining is a waft of savoury smoke blowing over the neighbours' garden. **Buy locally sourced charcoal (337)** from a supplier who grows wood sustainably. Avoid charcoal imported from distant places such as Indonesia: it's likely to have come from endangered forests, and to be bulked out with additives such as sand and clay to make it heavier – and therefore more expensive (it's also harder to light).

Don't use firelighter fluids or briquettes (338), which are made from petrol derivatives and can coat your food in harmful deposits. Instead use some scrunched-up old newspaper, dry twigs and, if necessary, a little kindling (small pieces of wood).

339 **Rocky patch** Rockeries are great for growing drought-resistant plants, and offer valuable shelter to creatures such as frogs, newts and toads. With this in mind, make sure you incorporate some nooks and crannies in any rock features you build in your garden.

340 **Natural shine** Make your own glass cleaner by mixing a little white vinegar in water in a refillable plastic spray bottle. As well as saving money, you'll avoid the isopropyl alcohol contained in most shop-bought products. This harms aquatic life and can affect the human nervous system, so you won't do yourself or your goldfish any good if you use it to clean the fish tank.

341 **Rescue a pet** Instead of buying a pet from a shop or breeder, visit an animal shelter and give a home to an animal in need.

342   **Wood is good** Sustainably forested timber is the best material for most household carpentry. Although particle boards such as MDF (Medium Density Fibreboard) and chipboard may appear easier to handle, they contain carcinogenic formaldehyde and should be worked with care. Why ignore the real thing?

343   **The greatest gift** Help to reduce the number of people dying prematurely from organ failure, or relying on high-tech hospital equipment, by donating your organs when you die. Ask your doctor for a donor card and let your family and close friends know your wish to donate.

344   **Steam scheme** When ironing avoid using the iron's steam setting; instead, spray water onto your clothes using a spray bottle. This greatly reduces your iron's energy use and stops its workings from clogging up with limescale.

345   **Spray away** Although aerosols no longer contain ozone-munching CFCs, many still use polluting hydrocarbon-based propellants. And since each can is made from a collection of valuable resources that can't be reused or recycled once the contents have been sprayed out, aerosols should be struck from the shopping list of any eco-conscious consumer. They can almost always be replaced with products in reusable pump containers.

346 **A wholesome night's sleep** Next time you need to buy a new mattress, look for one filled with natural materials such as horsehair, cotton, coir or coconut fibre. They conduct body moisture much more effectively than sweaty synthetic mattresses, don't sag in the middle, and can be produced with a fraction of the environmental impact of fabrics such as nylon. Sleep well!

347 **Computer age** Our growing dependency upon the computer is fast becoming an environmental scourge. More than 31 million PCs are thrown away worldwide each year. The plastic alone in each system requires 7 litres of crude oil to make, and when computers are discarded many of their components, including lead, nickel and cadmium, can become environmental hazards. Minimize this wastage by choosing a model that can be easily upgraded. When it's really no longer useful to you, **donate your computer to an organization that recycles IT equipment (348)** for resale or reuse by schools or charities.

349 **Exploratory exercise** Take your children on a bike ride. As
well as being a great way to bond with your kids while helping
them to get fit, a family bike ride can take you to parts of your
neighbourhood you'd never have known existed if you'd stayed
in your car. Even if there aren't dedicated bicycle lanes on the
roads around your home, it's likely there are some bike-friendly

trails that will lead you to interesting places. **Ask your national cycling association for maps of recommended routes (350).**

351 **Impeach the bleach** As well as blitzing the harmful bacteria in your toilet bowl, the caustic soda in bleach-based toilet cleaners kills the valuable organisms needed to digest waste in sewage plants, making the system inefficient and expensive. Instead, look for bleach-free, ecologically friendly toilet cleaners based on natural products. You can also **make your own toilet cleaner (352).** Flush the toilet to wet the sides, then tip a cup of borax around the bowl followed by a drizzle of white vinegar. Leave overnight, then scrub with a toilet brush, and flush.

353 **Organic gold mine** More than a third of the waste we put into our household bins is compostable organic matter. In a landfill this "green" material breaks down anaerobically to produce methane – a greenhouse gas some 23 times more potent than carbon dioxide. Separating out materials such as vegetable and fruit peel and cardboard packaging gives you free "fuel" for a compost heap, which will generate nutrient-rich matter to condition your soil and nourish your plants.

354   **Hidden menace** The flame retardant PBDE is often used to treat furniture, carpets and clothes. This very persistent synthetic compound accumulates in our bodies, and has been linked to hormone dysfunction. Make suppliers aware of your desire to avoid this compound by asking for PBDE-free products.

355   **Up, up and away** Use natural latex balloons to adorn your children's parties. A bunch of balloons drifting into the blue yonder can be a pretty spectacle, but once they've landed, the burst bubbles of foil or treated latex will linger as litter for years, and can choke cattle and wildlife. Natural latex is fully biodegradable – even if the odd balloon does end up in a tree rather than your compost bin.

356   **Dust to dust** Cremation releases a cocktail of toxins into the air. So opt for burial if you can, ideally in a woodland or farmland site, where your remains will nourish the earth you came from.

357   **Wedding list** Ask your friends and family to help set you up for a low-impact married life with gifts such as organic bed linen, solar-powered appliances or maybe even a mini wind turbine.

358   **Write an ethical will** Keep up your good work after you're gone by making a will that helps future generations look after the planet (see page 371). Leave bequests to organizations or charities you trust to make a difference on your behalf.

359   **Shattering success** The satisfying crash of glass being thrown into a bottle bank can be a great stress-buster. But don't get too carried away – make sure you put the right coloured glass in each section, or it will all have to be used to make green glass, which is of lower value than other colours.

360   **Does it work on bee stings?** Manuka honey has great antiseptic qualities – try using it to clean and soothe minor cuts, burns and grazes without the need for harsh chemical creams.

361   **Give a recycled gift** The recycling industry can only really work if there's a market for its products. Give a friend something beautiful or unusual made from recycled materials, such as a piece of jewellery or clothing, to remind them that there's more to recycled products than just toilet paper.

362 **Caring confetti** Rosebuds, petals, blossom, rice or biodegradable confetti made from recycled tissue paper bring magic to a just-married moment, then dissolve quickly.

---

363 **HOUSE AN OWL** Barn owls like to nest in hollow trees or hidden corners of old buildings. If you own a large garden, make it owl-friendly: install nesting boxes under the eaves of your home, leave old trees standing, and keep an area of grass uncut to provide a habitat for the small rodents on which owls prey.

---

364 **Mug's game** Keep a mug at work for all the hot drinks you need to fuel your day. You're a busy person – you deserve better than a mouthful of polystyrene or plastic.

365 **Over and over** Buy rewritable CDs and DVDs for files you need to copy or transport. If looked after properly, these disks can be reused hundreds of times, avoiding the need to buy packs and packs of single-use equivalents. Alternatively, **use a USB flash drive or your MP3 player (366)** to transport files.

367 **Take the easy option** Suggest to your employer that recycling bins (particularly for paper) be put closer to people's desks than the normal bins, so that even in the flurry of meeting a deadline recycling's the easier option.

368 **Permanent marker** Find a fountain pen you love and use it for life. A refillable pen with a nib that suits your writing style will not only make writing a more pleasant (and stylish) experience, but will avoid the waste of binning dozens of biros every year.

For scribbles when your fountain pen's not appropriate, **choose a mechanical pencil or refillable biro (369)**.

370 **Windows across the world** Next time you have a short meeting in a far-flung location, ask yourself whether you really need to be there in person. Video conferencing could save you a lot of time, and avoids environmentally damaging travel.

371 **Buy for keeps** Take advantage of low prices during the sales to invest in a few items you really need and want, but are normally outside your budget. A well-made, classic piece of clothing or furniture will last many times longer than a cheaper alternative.

372 **Respect your plastics** Despite its environmental problems, plastic can be very useful, and is impossible to avoid entirely in modern life. Make sure you're getting the most out of this valuable resource by reusing plastic packaging, then recycling it when it's no longer usable. Look for items made from PET (marked with a number 1 inside a triangle), which is the most easily recyclable plastic. Recycling just one PET bottle saves enough energy to power a 60-watt lightbulb for six hours.

373 **Tired eyes?** Before you buy another pot of gunk claiming to restore your natural sparkle, try putting the following on your closed eyes: cool wet tea bags (black, green, chamomile, elderflower, catnip or lavender tea are all soothing), cucumber slices, or cotton wool balls dampened with witch hazel. Lie down and relax for at least ten minutes to let the natural compounds do their stuff. If nothing else, you'll feel more rested.

374 **Go the extra mile** If you're going to the effort of saving bottles for recycling, make sure you first remove caps, corks and other additions, which contaminate potentially useful glass.

375 **THE GRASS IS GREENER** A petrol mower can produce as much pollution per hour as 40 cars! Instead, use an electric mower (ideally powered by electricity from a green tariff) – or a manual one, which will get you fit while you push it. Techno-gardeners should look out for self-guiding solar-powered models.

376 **Working lunch** Get together with colleagues to make food at lunchtime, and enjoy bonding with them over something more substantial than coffee. If necessary, ask your employer to provide some basic facilities for food preparation, so you don't have to rely on convenience food.

377 **Circular argument** No matter how shining your prose may be, there's no need to use brand-new envelopes to circulate internal notes and memos. Keep a supply of used envelopes to hand, and ask your colleagues to do the same.

378 **Eco poop scoop** To avoid adding to the plastic-bag mountain, scoop dog poop with bags made from biodegradable corn starch instead – these are available from many pet shops.

379 **Make love not pollution** When you've released yourself from Eros's embrace, don't throw your condom down the loo or it'll clog water-treatment facilities, or could end up on a riverbank or beach – or out at sea with its peers in a raft-like agglomeration. Instead, choose biodegradable latex condoms (most condoms are made of polyurethane) and put them in the bin afterwards.

380 **Can the cans** From canned pet food, gradually switch your dog or cat's diet to dried foods packaged in large cardboard or paper containers. They're lighter, saving on transportation costs and energy use, and the packaging is less resource- and energy-intensive (and can be added to your compost heap).

381 **Cool for cats** Conventional cat litter is based on clay or other minerals – products of environmentally damaging mining, and a heavy toxic burden in landfill sites once binned. If your cat has no outdoor access and really needs a litter tray, try biodegradable alternatives made of sawmill wastes, straw or hemp. They're lighter and can be flushed away or, preferably, buried in the soil of your garden.

382 **Use the right rocks** Make sure that your garden enhancements aren't despoiling a precious habitat elsewhere. Avoid using worn limestone and tufa as they may come from protected sites. Instead, use rocks dug from your own land or rejects from local building sites. Check where your pebbles come from and avoid ones removed from beaches. On a cumulative scale, such removal can damage rare habitats.

383 **Rag trade** Just because some of your oldest clothes are too worn out to be useful to anyone in their current incarnation, they needn't be thrown in the bin. Designers such as Oxfam's Traid Remade team in the UK are becoming increasingly adept at fashioning new items out of the best parts of unwanted old garments. And if your togs are beyond even that, they can still be shredded and rewoven into new items, via charity-run textile recycling schemes.

384 **On the piste** If you're a skiing fan, make sure your enjoyment of the slopes is of minimal threat to mountain areas – already suffering the early effects of climate change – by choosing a ski resort that's taking steps to minimize its environmental impact (see page 372). Initiatives to look out for include wind-powered ski lifts and car-pooling for staff and guests.

385 **Buy an ozone-friendly fridge** Next time your fridge needs replacing, look for a "greenfreeze" model, which cools using butane and propane rather than the ozone-munching CFCs, HFCs or HCFCs. "Greenfreeze" fridges also tend to be more energy-efficient than standard versions.

386 **Make your own logs** Turn your newspapers into free heating fuel using a "log maker" – a small gadget that turns your reading matter into compact pulp. Each newspaper will make roughly one log, which will burn for up to an hour. You can feed some versions of this device with paper shreddings, cardboard, wood chippings, dry leaves, twigs, chopped branches, wrapping paper, dry tea bags and junk mail. More simply, **roll newspaper sheets around a broomstick (387)** until the "log" is the desired thickness, then soak it thoroughly in water. Dry the log overnight, remove the broomstick, and use it like ordinary wood.

388 **Low-cost reading** Do you really need to pay through the nose for every word you read? Newspapers and magazines tend to be read only once before they're thrown away. Try cutting down your weekly reading stack by listening to the news on the radio, reading online or browsing the freebies in cafés and libraries.

389 **Cut out the legwork** If you're looking for an out-of-print book, save yourself wasted (and wasteful) journeys to second-hand bookshops by visiting a website (see page 373) that allows you to search a global network of book dealers.

390 **Career change** If your old clothes, sheets and towels are too worn out to grace a charity shop, try cutting them into squares to use as washable cloths for cleaning floors and other surfaces, dusting, and wiping up spills.

391 **DO A HOME DRAUGHT AUDIT** Hold a lit candle next to window and door frames. If the flame flickers, there's a gap that needs to be plugged.

392 **Better battery habits** Most batteries leak toxic metals such as mercury, nickel and cadmium when you throw them away. So choose rechargeable alkaline manganese batteries, which are free from toxic heavy metals, invest in a battery charger (ideally, a solar-powered one) and teach everyone in your family how to use it.

393 **Faithful friend** Exotic pets are often captured from endangered wild populations and imported illegally. They can be hard to care for, and so often end up dumped in the wild, where they can wreak havoc on the local ecosystem. Build a more lasting relationship with a dog or cat from your local animal shelter.

394 **Definitely not cool** Dumped fridges and freezers are not only an eyesore but an ecological hazard, as they can contain ozone-depleting CFCs and HCFCs. At the end of your appliance's life, take it to a dedicated recycling point, where these chemicals can be professionally removed.

395 **Elect to vote** It can often feel like we have little say over the way our world is run. But if you live in a democracy, your vote counts! At election time, find out which candidate is offering the best deal for the planet and give them your support. Better still, contact your local political representative right now and let them know what you'd like them to do on your behalf.

396   **Don't be foiled** Aluminium production is a resource- and energy-intensive process. So use foil sparingly, and where possible wash and fold it for reuse. When it's no longer usable, make sure you recycle it.

When there's no option but to use aluminium foil (for example, for covering food while roasting), make sure you **use a foil made from 100 per cent recycled aluminium (397)**. Recycling aluminium uses a twentieth of the energy needed to smelt the virgin metal from ore.

398   **Veggie vacation** If you'd like to eat more vegetarian meals but are stuck for inspiration, why not put yourself in the hands of some experts on a course, tour or even holiday focused on vegetarian or vegan food (see page 372)? As well as giving you all kinds of appetizing recipe ideas, they'll show you how to derive the full range of nutrients from a plant-based diet.

399   **Pond life** Make a pond in your garden and create a whole
new ecosystem right on your doorstep. Make sure it has gently
sloping sides to enable small animals to escape if they fall in (and
a fence around it if you have small children). A combination of

shallow and deep areas planted with a mix of aquatic plants will provide habitats for a range of creatures, who'll quickly colonize their new home if it's left undisturbed for a few months.

400 **Happy re-tyre-ment** When they're no longer roadworthy, old tyres can be turned into new products such as safe surfaces for playgrounds, mousemats, or notebook covers. Support this reuse industry by buying a tyre-based gift for a car-mad friend.

401 **Comfort food** When you've finished using your oven, open the door and let the warm air help heat your home.

402 **Crafty wrapping** Use up offcuts of material from curtain- or dress-making or old unwanted clothes to make a beautiful, personalized bag to wrap a gift. If it's well made, it may last longer than the gift inside! Perhaps even cannier, **look for "wrapping" that's a gift in itself (403)**, such as a brightly coloured tea towel or scarf, or a beautiful storage box. These can all contain smaller gifts and will be treasured in their own right. Add a (reusable) ribbon to perfect the waste-free presentation of your gift.

404 **Fact of life** Your one moggie might not have much of an environmental impact, but if it produced even a couple of litters, it could end up at the head of a feline family tree of thousands, which would make a severe dent in the local population of small creatures. Do the responsible thing: get your cat neutered.

405 **Outdoor education** Encourage your local school to establish a conservation area in its grounds. This could simply be an area of land left to regenerate into a variety of natural habitats, or a more diverse patch incorporating a working garden. Either way, it will be an important teaching resource. Offer your time to help establish and manage it.

406 **Get behind the bike shelter** In Denmark 60 per cent of children cycle to school. Encourage your local school to move toward this target by asking them to provide secure bike shelters for pupils and staff.

407 **Reinvent the wheel** We get through 200 million car tyres a year in western Europe alone – and they take up to 400 years to begin decomposing. Help to reduce this rubber mountain by retreading your tyres when they wear down. This process is carried out to strict safety standards and uses only a fraction of the energy it takes to replace the tyre.

If your car does need new shoes, ask your garage to **fit eco-friendly tyres (408)**, which use organic ingredients such as corn starch in place of non-renewable chemicals.

409   **Good news about hydrogen** Many experts believe that hydrogen will play a key role in building a diversified energy system based on renewable power supplies, as it can be used as a medium for carrying and storing energy. This could help even out the intermittency of some renewable sources – for example, enabling energy from sunlight to be stored for use overnight.

Major car manufacturers are developing vehicles with electric motors powered by hydrogen fuel cells. This technology has the potential to drastically reduce pollution: the only thing that comes out of the tailpipe of a hydrogen car is water vapour.

At the moment, the most efficient way to produce hydrogen is by burning natural gas, a fossil fuel. However, scientists are working hard to find a way to enable large-scale production using renewable energy. Keep up with the latest developments.

410 **Traffic filter** Travelling along the side of the road, cyclists are actually exposed to two to four times less pollution than people inside vehicles stuck bumper to bumper in a traffic jam. But to give added protection to your lungs while cycling, get yourself a face mask to cover your nose and mouth.

---

411 **SOMETHING FOR NOTHING** Look out for gadgets such as radios and chargers – for everything from mobile phones to laptops – that run on solar power and/or wind-up mechanisms.

---

412 **Pool your resources** If everyone who regularly drives to work on their own were to share a ride even just once a week, traffic volumes would fall by 10–15 per cent.

413 **Two-mile rule** Up to half of journeys made by car in developed countries are less than two miles long. Sadly, this is when car engines are at their least efficient and most polluting. Make it a rule to walk or cycle journeys of less than two miles. You may need to invest in some waterproof clothing and decent paniers, but your legs and heart will thank you in the long run.

If you're not sure that your legs are up to regular cycling, **try an electric bicycle (414)** instead. Quiet and clean (especially if powered using renewable energy), it lets you glide through traffic jams at speeds of up to 15 miles an hour. If storage space is your problem, at home or at work, **buy a folding bicycle (415)**.

416 **Take great strides** Try strapping some springy "powerizer" stilts onto your calves to increase your stride length dramatically. Once you've mastered the rocking motion, you'll be able to leap forward around five metres with a single bound, enabling you to make journeys on foot in a fraction of the usual time.

417 **Take a meal on the wild side** You may be surprised how much food is growing all around you. If you're uncertain what to look for, carry a good identification guide to the wild plants in your region. Select young, fresh plants from unpolluted areas, and don't take more than will quickly grow back. You could try making wild garlic pesto, elderflower wine, blackberry jam, nettle soup, crab apple jelly, horseradish sauce, or sage tea … Your food will be guaranteed free from pesticides and preservatives – fresh and very local.

418 **Flushed with excess** There's no good reason for using a 9-litre flush of carefully processed drinking water to dispose of anything that could go into your dustbin, recycling bin or compost heap. Apart from the terrible waste of a precious resource, when flushed down the loo items such as tampons, condoms and razorblades can cause blockages in the sewage system, and end up in waterways or on the beach. Wouldn't you rather feel sand between your toes?

419 **Recycle your cycle** If you're upgrading your bike, don't scrap the old one. Your local bike shop may offer a part-exchange scheme, and even if your bike's too much of a wreck to be of any value to them, it's still likely to be useful for parts. Bicycle recycling projects are often community run and provide jobs for people out of work. Some schemes collect, mend and ship second-hand bicycles and parts to Africa (see page 373).

420 **Make the plastic bag history** We use 8 per cent of the world's oil supply to produce plastic, including billions of plastic bags each year. Not only is this a huge waste of resources, but it results in lots of unnecessary long-term landfill, as it's believed that each bag will take up to 500 years to decompose. Limit the number of plastic bags you need by packing carefully and reusing them. And **ask shops to provide biodegradable bags (421)** made from corn starch. Better still, don't use plastic bags at all – **keep a couple of string, jute** (see page 147) **or canvas bags to hand (422)** instead.

423 **Re-label your envelopes** Rather than throwing all the envelopes you receive away after a single use, open them carefully so they can be reused by sticking a label over the original address. A number of charities produce special self-adhesive labels made from recycled paper. These are big enough to fold over the top of the envelope, so you don't need any tape or staples to seal it.

424 **Make your own lemonade** You may not be able to grow your own lemons or sugar, but you can still mix juice from organic Fairtrade lemons together with some sugar and filtered water to make a drink that's cheaper, healthier and much, much tastier than any you can buy.

425 **Plant a wildflower meadow** Rather than having a large, manicured lawn, try planting an area of your garden with a wildflower mix. Wildflower meadows grow best on poor soil, so don't require any fertilizers (or weedkillers, of course), need cutting only twice a year, are gorgeously colourful, and attract butterflies, birds and bees.

426   **In praise of jute** Otherwise known as hessian or burlap, the fibrous plant jute needs far less water than cotton, and little or no fertilizer and pesticide. It has many uses – from reusable carrier bags to curtains, carpets, and matting to prevent soil erosion.

427   **Chop on wood** So-called "antibacterial" plastic chopping boards have become popular in recent years. But there is concern that the triclosan impregnated in these and similar household products can foster antibiotic-resistant strains of bacteria. There's no need to introduce this potentially risky substance into your home. Far better to harness the natural bactericidal properties of wood: a regularly scrubbed, sustainably sourced wooden chopping board can't be beaten.

428   **Don't be a butthead** Once you've stubbed out your cigarette, make sure you put the butt in a bin. As well as being an eyesore, these tiny pieces of litter can choke birds and animals, or poison them with tobacco and tar if they manage to swallow them.

429   **Open and shut case** Line your drawers beautifully using unused ends of wallpaper rolls.

430 **Festive glow** Christmas lights aren't the most essential way to use energy, but the festive period would be far duller without them. To get the most striking effect for the least electricity, **try hanging LED (Light Emitting Diode) lights (431)**. These 0.4-watt bulbs use up to 100 times less energy than some traditional Christmas lights, and last up to 100,000 hours when used indoors. And, unlike the energy-hungry conventional versions, if one of the LED lights burns out, the rest of the strand will stay lit, meaning that there's never a problem identifying the faulty bulb.

Decorative lights designed for indoors generally use less energy than outdoor versions, so if you want to share your bonhomie with your neighbours, **string lights around the inside of your windows (432)** rather than outside.

433 **Show your cans who's boss** Recycling just one aluminium can saves enough energy to run a TV set for three hours. Help make the process even more efficient by crushing your cans before collection. This means that they take up less space, which reduces the number of trips required to take them to the recycling plant. (The same principle applies to plastic bottles.)

Crushing cans with your own strength is a great way to release frustration (as long as you take care with sharp edges), but you can also **get a can crusher (434)** – a simple gadget that makes short work of even the sturdiest cans.

435 **Get going!** Drive off as soon as you start your car's engine. Modern engines don't need time to warm up, so idling creates unnecessary pollution and mechanical wear.

436 **Be an anti-litter bug** Pick up at least one piece of litter each day and put it in a bin (or recycle it if appropriate). This might seem like an inconsequential action, but if everyone on your street did the same, there would be skip-loads less litter blowing around your front door.

437 **Never pour engine oil down the drain!** Instead, ask your local petrol station or recycling depot whether they accept it for re-refining. This process filters out toxic heavy metals such as nickel, cadmium and lead and leaves the oil as good as new (see pages 270–271). A single litre of oil poured down the drain can contaminate millions of litres of water.

438 **TAKE YOUR CHILDREN TO AN ORGANIC FARM** Many organic farms actively encourage visitors to explore their land on nature trails or simply to look and learn. There should be plenty to spot – as well as the obvious crops and herds, one British study has shown that organic farms contain 85 per cent more plant species, 33 per cent more bats, 17 per cent more spiders and 5 per cent more birds than non-organic ones.

---

439 **Buy recycled stationery** Recycled paper not only saves trees, but requires a lot less energy to produce than virgin paper. It's also free from chlorine-based bleach and petrochemical-based optical brighteners, which, when they enter waterways, can damage plants and animals.

440 **Invest in an ethical pension fund** You'll get old a lot more gracefully if you retire ethically. Make sure that your monthly contributions are funding something positive by choosing a fund that invests according to stringent, clearly stated ethical criteria.

441 **Buy an acre of rainforest** Tropical rainforests are the Earth's oldest and most complex land-based ecosystem, and contain half of its wildlife and at least two-thirds of its plant species. They play a vital role in regulating global climate and preventing soil erosion, are home to indigenous cultures, and provide a rich source of ingredients for medicines. But an area the size of Wales is being cut down every year in the Amazon alone to make way for cattle ranching, logging, plantations, mining, oil exploration and dams. Do your bit by "buying" a section of this vital ecosystem (see page 370) to ensure it's protected in perpetuity.

442 **High-IQ battery charging** Some chargers continue to feed energy into batteries even when they're fully charged. To avoid wasting energy and reducing battery life by overcharging, look for an "intelligent" charger that uses the "delta v" or "delta t" detection technique to sense when charging is complete, and then reduces its energy output to a trickle. That way you don't have to be around to unplug it once your batteries are topped up.

443 **Clean, hot hobs** If you have an electric hob, clean it regularly so that the rings can work efficiently.

444 **Detox your sex life** Those who like to accessorize between the sheets should beware that many plastic sex toys contain phthalates, which studies suggest can damage the liver, the kidneys, the lungs and the reproductive system, as well as having nasty environmental impacts. Whatever your fancy, greener alternatives exist, from all-natural lubricants to animal-free bondage gear. There are even solar-powered vibrators – cleverly designed to maintain their charge in the dark!

445 **A simpler life** If you want to reduce your impact on the world, concentrate on simplifying your life (see page 372). Make an effort to reduce the number of things you own, keeping only belongings that you use or enjoy regularly. This will probably feel difficult to begin with, but by developing this mindset, you'll naturally buy less and create less waste in the future.

446 **Foster an ape** Our closest relatives, the apes, are under increasing threat as we hunt them and plunder their habitats. By joining a fostering programme, you can support charities that look after the orphans found wandering after their mothers have been killed for bushmeat or taken for the illegal pet trade.

447 **Take your time** Rushing often makes "convenience" options unavoidable – jumping into a taxi rather than walking to a meeting, or grabbing a packaged sandwich rather than eating fresh food for lunch. This hectic approach often carries a hefty price tag – both for our wallets and the environment – and can be detrimental to our health and happiness. Plan ahead as much as you can, and be realistic about how much you can fit into the day. You may have to do less. But try to do it properly – and enjoy the ride!

448 **Be a fruit and veg traditionalist** Always favouring the most productive and disease-resistant option, most supermarkets stock a tiny selection of the huge range of fruit and vegetable varieties traditionally grown. About 90 per cent of lettuce and 80 per cent of tomato varieties have been lost in this focus on profitability, depriving us of a host of wonderful flavours, and limiting the biological diversity which allows crops to adapt naturally to cope with changing growing conditions. Buck the trend and tantalize your tastebuds by buying and growing as many different types of fruit and vegetable as you can.

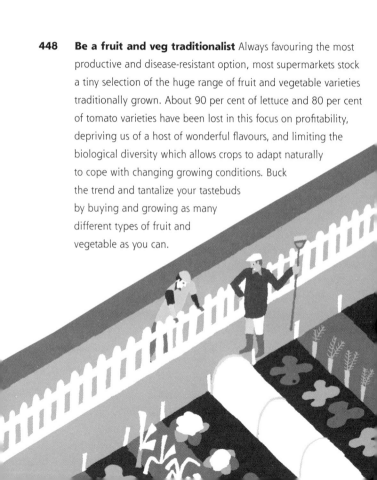

449   **How big is your footprint?** Work through an ecological footprint quiz (see page 370) to estimate how much productive land and water is used to support your lifestyle, and see how that compares to people in other parts of the world. You may find that you're already living quite lightly, but you're more likely to get a shock – if everyone on Earth lived like the average Westerner, we'd need more than three planets to support us.

---

450   **WALK YOUR TALK** Don't just talk about changing the world – get on with it! Actions speak louder than words. As Mahatma Gandhi said, we must "be the change we want to see in the world".

---

451   **The sea is not a litter bin** The oceans may be vast, but they're becoming clogged with our rubbish. Much of the waste we produce takes centuries to break down, and causes untold environmental damage in the process. Explain to your children – if they don't know already – that throwing rubbish off a boat or a pier is just as bad as dropping it in the street.

452 **Outward bound** Host your child's birthday party in the woods. Challenge the unruly mob to make dens that will shelter them from the elements. Tap into their animal instincts and watch them become absorbed in the natural world around them.

453 **Birdwatching** Help your children to survey the birds in your garden: put a range of foods (see page 205) on a bird table and spend ten minutes each day counting how many birds visit in that period. As you make your garden more attractive to different species and put food out more regularly, you should notice an increase in the number of feathered visitors. A basic identification book will help the kids work out who's who.

454 **Make your own popcorn** Heat a little oil in a large pan. Once the oil is hot, cover the bottom of the pan with a thin layer of maize kernels and put a lid on. Shake the pan from time to time to stop the kernels burning, and take it off the heat once the popping sounds have subsided. Add a little salt or sugar for a cheap, low-impact snack that's healthier than additive-laced commercial equivalents.

455 Feeling clucky? If you have a little outdoor space, it's very easy to keep a few chickens to provide you with daily eggs. They eat almost anything except citrus peel, so you can feed them all your kitchen scraps, ensuring they get a nutritious (organic if you're eating it) and hormone-free diet that will be recycled into delicious, fresh, food-mile-free eggs for you and your family. As an added benefit, chickens enjoy foraging for numerous garden pests, including slugs and snails.

456 Natural deodorant Many commercial deodorants contain aluminium, which can be absorbed through the skin, affect internal organs and increase the risk of blood poisoning. They also tend to be highly perfumed and packaged. Instead, go for a natural "crystal" deodorant made from mineral salts. One of these lasts for years, so minimizing packaging and transportation. Or for a DIY alternative, **try patting baking soda onto damp skin after washing (457).**

458 Clean, green shaving The average (cleanshaven) man spends five months of his life shaving. So make sure this time-consuming ritual has minimal environmental impact: first of all by choosing a razor that requires you to replace only the blade head when the blade gets blunt, not the whole body of the razor. **Use a razor-cartridge sharpener (459)** to extend the life of your blade: this will reduce the number of disposable blade heads you get through by up to 75 per cent. Even better, **shave the old-fashioned way (460)** with a straight razor and hard soap. The blades are permanent, offer the closest shave, and a good vegetable-based soap is better for the environment.

If the cut-throat route seems too daunting, **try a rechargeable electric razor (461)**, which, aside from its potentially toxic hardware makeup, is by no means the worst option. A good model can last for years and provides a close shave without highly packaged and processed creams or gels.

---

462 **DRAUGHT-DODGING** Stop heat sneaking out and make your home more comfortable by fixing draught excluders (either foam or longer-lasting metal strips) around doors, windows and letter boxes. Plug any gaps between skirting boards and the floor with wooden beading.

463   **Down in the basement** If you have a cellar, installing a layer of underfloor insulation will cut heat loss from your home by up to a quarter, and create a much cosier basement.

464   **Get off the treadmill** Exercise machines burn up a phenomenal amount of electricity (ten treadmills in the average gym use about 13,500 kilowatt hours of electricity a month – enough to run a hairdryer nonstop for more than a year), and the gyms that house them are also heavy consumers of air conditioning and laundry to mop up your sweat. So put your gym membership on hold and instead, when the weather's fine, take your dog or a friend for a run in the park. You may even find you still enjoy it when it's raining.

465   **Vintage style** The quality of workmanship on vintage clothes is often much higher than on modern mass-produced clothing, so not only will classic clothing generally cost less, it'll also last longer than new items. And your style will be unique!

466   **Love your bling?** To help avoid the environmental problems associated with mining metal and gems, buy jewellery made from recycled precious metals and stones, or dust off old pieces handed down by your grandparents – perhaps commissioning a jeweller to transform them into radiant recycled classics.

467 **Kinder diamonds** More than four million people have been killed in conflicts surrounding the sale of illegal diamonds. Buying an ethical, conflict-free diamond ensures that your money doesn't fund a regime responsible for illegal operations, wars and human-rights abuses. In fact, if you purchase your diamond through an organization that specializes in ethically sourced diamonds, some of the money may go toward helping victims of the cruelty that results from the competition for these precious stones.

468 **Reincarnate your mobile** Improved technology and increasingly fashionable and appealing designs mean we update our mobile phones ever more regularly. The discarded old ones can leach a cocktail of environmentally damaging metals and flame retardants into the air and groundwater. So be sure either to return the old phone to your retailer for recycling or donate it to a charity that collects them for reuse.

469   **No smoke without fire** Avoid burning rubbish in your garden: it can release clouds of harmful chemicals and carbon dioxide. Limit bonfires to wood, leaves and other organic waste if you really can't keep your hands out of the matchbox. But it's much easier and more beneficial to dispose of organic matter on a compost heap.

470   **Count the calories** You may be used to thinking about the amount of energy, or calories, that the food you eat provides you with. But have you thought about how much energy goes into growing and processing your food? The toll can quickly add up: modern food production and distribution systems can use up to 15 times more energy than the resulting food actually provides you with. To cut the production calories, try to buy as many fresh, unprocessed foods as possible.

471   **Greenhouse effect** You can make mini-greenhouses out of plastic bottles. Simply cut off the base, and use the remaining "cloche" as a starter home for seedlings. It'll create a warm microclimate, and keep slugs and snails at bay through the plants' early months.

472 **KEEP THE PRESSURE UP** Maintaining the appropriate pressure in your vehicle's tyres will help to minimize its fuel use.

---

473 **Bring dead wood back to life** Rather than sending waste wood from your garden to landfill, try breaking it into small pieces and adding it to your compost heap, where it will provide valuable fibre.

474 **Lolly labels** Put your children's wooden ice-lolly sticks to good use by using them to label plants. Once the plants have grown large enough that they no longer need tags, you can bury the sticks in the soil, where they'll decompose to provide useful fibre.

475 **Bricks work** Keep hold of old bricks: they have masses of uses in the garden – from supporting a water butt or planter to making a raised bed or barbecue stand.

476 **Hot spot** Try to position your compost heap or wormery (see page 215) in a sunny spot. The warmer it is, the faster the micro-organisms it contains will do their work. Just make sure you turn the composting material over regularly, especially in very hot weather, to keep it evenly damp and aerated.

477 **Make a mini-pool** If you haven't got space for a pond, try filling a container, such as an old enamel or ceramic sink, with water and putting it in a quiet place in your garden. Add a few stones at one end, so that frogs, toads and other creatures can get in and out easily.

478 **Keep pests at bay** Rather than resorting to child- and environment-unfriendly store-bought chemical solutions when faced with insects in your kitchen, try some naturally sourced alternatives instead. Many insects have an aversion to basil; ants don't like cucumber peel or peppermint; and weevils can be kept out of your flour and cereals by adding bay leaves.

479 **Save your candles for next year, and the one after ...** Birthday cakes with candles aren't a serious contributor to climate change – even if you're celebrating a hundredth birthday with the right number of candles. But just in case you're worried, blow out the candles and reuse them next time, with their tops nicked off. On a green planet maybe we'll all live to be a hundred.

480 **Drain-busting** Clear your drains with a mixture of baking soda and vinegar in boiling water, using a plunger for extra power. This solution is much cheaper than commercial drain cleaners, which contain corrosive and toxic ingredients, such as sodium hydroxide, hydrochloric acid and petroleum distillates, which damage aquatic life and make water more expensive to treat.

481 **Keep a weather eye** Before you water the garden, check the local weather forecast. If rain's in the offing, there's no need to give your plants a drink.

482 **Shine on** To give silver cutlery a natural polish, put a sheet of aluminium foil into a plastic or glass bowl. Sprinkle with salt and baking soda and fill the bowl with warm water. Soak your silver items in the bowl and the tarnish will migrate to the foil. Dry and buff your treasures, and they're ready for use, with no nasty chemical residues to spoil the flavour of your next family meal.

483 **Brass rubbing** Polish brass fittings the natural way by rubbing them with half a lemon sprinkled with salt. Let the metal dry and then buff it with a cloth.

484 **Strike a light!** One of the simplest ways to get rid of a bad smell – in the toilet, for example – is to strike a match and let the flame burn for a moment. This miraculously eliminates nasty odours without the need to mask them with another, often highly packaged and processed scent. Just make sure you extinguish the match properly before you put it in the bin!

485 **CREDIT-WORTHY** Do some good every time
you flex your plastic by using a credit card
that makes a small donation to your favourite
charity whenever you use it. Even better, do
this good work yourself: **look for ways to
reduce unnecessary spending (486)**, and
give a decent proportion of the money you
save directly to charity.

487 **Let's hear it for latex paint**
Because they're water-based,
latex paints contain fewer hazardous
chemicals than oil-based paints, and
don't require dangerous solvents
for thinning or brush cleaning. They
perform at least as well as their oil-based
equivalents for most indoor and outdoor jobs.

488 **Recycle leftover paint** If you've got various tins of leftover paint, mix them together to make a primer for your next paint job. But don't try to combine different types (such as latex and oil-based paints) or you'll end up with an unusable gunk.

489 **Love your brushes** Take care of your paintbrushes and they'll last much longer. Buy good-quality brushes and clean them carefully. When you've finished painting, first wipe any excess paint onto newspaper. Then, for oil brushes, use a small amount of white spirit, and wipe with more newspaper. For emulsion brushes, use hot water and a spot of detergent. Keep brushes used for black paint just for black paint jobs.

490 **Preparation is all** Calculate the surface area to be painted before you start decorating so you buy only as much paint as you need to cover it.

491 **Hook your carpets down** If you're having new carpets fitted, ask the fitters to use physical fastening "hook and loop" strips or dry adhesives like peel-and-stick strips rather than commercial adhesives, which can be a major source of volatile organic compounds (see page 186).

492 **Buy reclaimed wooden furniture** An area of ancient woodland the size of a football pitch is destroyed every two seconds. Make sure your home isn't contributing to the destruction by buying furniture that's either second hand or made from reclaimed wood.

493 **Look for leaks** A significant proportion of the water processed for human use is lost before it reaches our homes and offices. Help your water company get on top of this problem by reporting any leaks or unusual puddles. And do your bit by fixing any leaking pipes in and around your own home.

494 **Foods of love** The sustainable methods used to farm oysters make this well-known aphrodisiac one of the most environmentally sound, so go ahead and indulge yourself. **Stay in the mood with ginkgo biloba (495)**, believed to help with male impotence, and ginseng, said to boost stamina.

496 **GET TO KNOW YOUR LOWLIFE NEIGHBOURS**
To show your children just how many creatures share your garden, sink a clean jam jar, with its lid off, into a hole in the ground and leave it out on a warm dry night. Next morning, introduce your kids to the beetles, woodlice and other minibeasts who've stumbled in, before tipping them out to resume their business.

497 **Office clear-out?** Every corporate revamp releases a stream of perfectly serviceable desks, filing cabinets and other office furniture that may well be gold dust to community groups, churches, shelters or schools. So ask if they'd like some new kit before everything goes to the dump.

498 **Keep on keeping on** Changing to a low-impact lifestyle can feel like a drag – the constant weighing-up of choices that you used to make without a thought can take its toll. When motivation's hard to come by, and you're feeling more inclined to throw in the towel than check whether it's made from organic cotton, it's time to give yourself a boost. If you've been keeping one, reach for your green journal (see pages 53–54) and **congratulate yourself on your planet-saving achievements (499)**.

Your eco-stamina will also improve if you give yourself something specific to aim for, so **set new green goals (500)** for you and your family. When you achieve your targets, **give the whole family a reward (501)** – perhaps a picnic, nature trail or day at the beach.

502 **Going, going, gone!** If you need to raise money for a good cause, why not auction people's skills or some special experiences rather than physical items that may well end up as waste. For example: a romantic serenade, a week in someone's holiday cottage, tea with someone famous, a harp lesson, a trip to your local TV studios, a luxury home-delivered organic breakfast. Use your imagination and watch the bids go sky high.

503 **Cop shop** Police auctions can be a great source of second-hand bargains in very good condition. Items for sale include electrical and household goods, gardening equipment, bicycles and unclaimed lost property.

504 **Spot-on spot treatment** Almost all of us experience acne at some point in our lives. While the uncannily bad timing of the eruptions may seem scary, the noxious concoctions we blithely dab on our perturbing pimples are a lot more frightening. Treatments based on organically grown essential oils (such as tea tree, which has anti-bacterial and anti-inflammatory properties) are much healthier for the environment, the people who cultivate them, and the people who use them.

505 **Recycled worktops** Next time you refurbish your home or workplace, put some disposable packaging into long-term employment by specifying work surfaces, table tops or doors to be made out of sheets of recycled plastic. The unique patterns created by melting yogurt pots, plastic cups or even mobile phones provide a beautiful focal point, as well as durable surfaces that last for years.

506 A FAIR EXCHANGE
Children usually grow
out of clothes and
other paraphernalia well
before they're worn out. Rather
than buying everything new,
lend, borrow and swap equipment
with friends whose children are
older or younger than yours. You can
also pick up second-hand bargains in good
condition from charity shops and on auction
or exchange websites (see page 371).

---

507 **Clean sweep** Use a broom instead of a hose to clean your
driveway, patio and paths. If necessary, use a quick sluice of water
(ideally once it's been used to do the washing up) to wash away
any remaining dust once you've finished sweeping.

508 **Focused organic shopping** World consumption of chemical
pesticides and fertilizers is exploding – from 30 million tonnes
a year in 1960 to 140 million four decades later – and this

trend is unlikely to stop unless consumers demand it. If you can't get hold of a full range of organic groceries, or have a limited budget, prioritize buying organic items that in conventional agriculture are particularly laden with chemicals. Try always to buy organic bread (and other wheat products), apples, celery, strawberries, peaches, grapes, spinach and pears to avoid the worst chemical overloads.

509 **Travel light** Take nothing but pictures, leave nothing but footprints.

510 **Do it right** Want to make sure your DIY project will have minimal environmental impact? Ask the experts for help. Visit a specialist eco store (online or in person) to find out about the growing number of environmental building products and techniques available.

511 **One person's junk ...** If you're having a clear-out, hold a yard sale or hire a pitch at a car boot sale. By decluttering in this way, your unwanted items will go to people who have use for them, rather than just ending up at the dump.

512 **Don't kill with kindness** Feeding bread to ducks and other waterfowl is a popular way to spend time in the park, but it may do more harm than good. The bread makes the ducks feel full, but doesn't give them the nutrients they require, leaving them vulnerable to illness.

513 **Keep it sleek** Modern cars are designed to be aerodynamic, slipping through the air with minimum friction and maximum fuel efficiency. Roof racks have exactly the opposite effect – so don't keep them on the car unless you're planning to use them, especially if you're going on a long, high-speed journey.

514 **Greener golfing** Golf is good for getting outdoors, but it's not always great for the environment. So try taking steps to reduce the ecological impact of your fun on the greens. A good place to start would be to **join a "green" golf club (515)**. It should have features such as naturally weed-resistant grass to minimize pesticide use, and a watering system that uses reclaimed water. For the benefit of your health as well as the environment, **walk the course instead of using a golf cart (516)**. If you need to use a cart, keep to the designated paths to avoid straying onto natural habitats for wildlife, and urge your club to replace its fleet with electric-powered ones, if they haven't already. And while you're at it, **let your club know you'd rather play on brown grass (517)** during periods of low rainfall than on needlessly watered fairways. The grass will soon recover when it starts to rain again.

518 **Monitor your car's appetite** If your car starts doing fewer miles to the gallon than normal, its engine may need tuning. So calculate your miles per gallon each time you fill your tank (divide the number of miles travelled since the last fill-up by the number of gallons purchased this time). If your fuel economy drops significantly, and there's no other obvious explanation (such as an increase in stop-start urban driving), get your car checked out as soon as possible.

519   Counter-top baking If you often bake small meals, consider investing in a toaster oven, which uses less than half as much energy as a conventional oven.

---

520   FLY A KITE! Get the whole family outdoors enjoying the power of the wind. You'll get fit, improve your coordination, and have fun. Buy a second-hand kite or make your own (see page 372).

---

521   Heating at your fingertips If you have a simple mechanical thermostat, consider replacing it with a programmable digital model. This will give you greater control over your heating, enabling you to save energy without sacrificing comfort.

522 **Make the most of your fan** Surprising as it may seem, if you live in a continental climate it may be worth using your ceiling fan in the winter as well as the summer. By reversing the direction of the blades in the winter, warmer air is pushed down, causing heat to be distributed throughout the house, which means that your heating system doesn't have to work as hard.

523 **Do you really need a fur coat?** Traditionally seen as a sign of wealth, fur coats are a costly way to keep warm in more ways than one. Most real fur coats use pelts from fur farms, where animals are often kept in inhumane conditions. Unlike most "natural" products, real fur is also bad for the environment: it requires a huge amount of energy to produce and is processed with carcinogenic formaldehyde and chromium.

Fake fur is little better. Although involving no cruelty to animals, it is made from nylon, which is manufactured from oil – about a third of a barrel for the average coat – producing toxic nitrous oxide emissions along the way.

If you can't resist the allure of fur, the lowest-impact options are to **acquire a second-hand or vintage garment (524)**, or buy a new item made from recycled pelts.

525 **Give leather shoes the boot** Next time you need to buy some new footwear, look for alternatives to virgin leather. Around 95 per cent of leather products are chrome-tanned, producing waste certified as "hazardous". Vegan shoes are made from a variety of non-leather materials, but bear in mind that if they're plastic-based they're likely to have a high environmental impact. Instead, **look for shoes made from recycled materials (526)**, which are just beginning to move from worthy to desirable. Look for shoes with soles made from recycled rubber (often from car tyres) and uppers made of everything from leather rescued from old car seats to cotton from reclaimed jeans and surplus military jackets.

Whatever material they're made from, **get maximum mileage out of your shoes (527)** by looking after them properly. Invest in some shoe trees (ideally wooden) to help your shoes retain their shape, clean them regularly, particularly if they're leather (apart from making them look smarter, this will help keep the leather watertight), and have them re-soled and re-heeled whenever they begin to wear down.

528 **Runny nose?** Use a handkerchief rather than paper tissues to blow your nose. Not only will this save trees, but the (ideally organic) cotton will be kinder to your nose than the wood fibres in tissues.

529 **Dip into a skip** House clearances and refurbishments generate lots of goodies destined for landfill that still have plenty of mileage in them. Look out for building activity in your area – it could yield a sink, sofa or sideboard perfect for your home. Be sure to ask before you take items if they're on someone's driveway. Their previous owners will usually be delighted you're lightening their load.

530 **Need a new carpet?** If you're planning to replace your carpet, look into recycled versions. Their hard-wearing surface is particularly good for high-traffic areas such as offices and hallways. And rather than lobbing it into landfill, **recycle your old carpet (531)**. There are companies that will take worn-out carpet away and process it into new carpet, as well as all kinds of other products – from parking barriers to car components.

532   **SEE THE TREES FOR THE WOOD** Mahogany and teak are beautiful, high-quality tropical hardwoods that take many decades to mature and often come from endangered forests. If you need a hardwood, look for an approved-source scheme, or try a responsible company that plants and sustainably harvests its own.

533 **PVC-exclusion zone** PVC is a source of hormone-disrupting chemicals and is potentially carcinogenic. Make sure it doesn't sneak into your home in wallpaper, shower curtains, water pipes or other plastic components. Carefully read descriptions on packaging, and if you're having building work done, insist on using alternative materials.

534 **Strip your paint safely** Steer clear of solvent-based products. As well as giving you a headache, burning your skin and discolouring wood, they damage the environment at the time of manufacture and point of use. The high levels of volatile organic compounds (VOCs) they contain contribute to the depletion of the ozone layer and may be carcinogenic. To avoid these unpleasant side effects, use water-based paint-strippers. They're pH-neutral, biodegradable and much more pleasant to use.

535 **Looking for unique wallpaper?** Try using sheets of unwanted music, pages from your favourite magazines or spreads from the newspapers you most respect to create one-of-a-kind, striking décor. If you get tired of looking at any areas, simply paper over them in an ever-evolving montage.

536   **Stay sharp** Invest in a sharpening stone or other device to keep your kitchen knives razor sharp. Used regularly, this will keep good-quality knives in perfect form indefinitely. So no need to keep forking out to satisfy your carrot-chopping (or knife-throwing) habit.

537   **Timber trouble** Be wary of timber with a pale green stain: this is a sign that the wood has been pressure treated with the toxic compound chromated copper arsenate (CCA) to protect it against rot and pests. Although the sale of CCA-treated wood was severely curtailed in the EU in 2004, most existing fencing, decking and wooden outdoor furniture will have been constructed from it. On no account burn CCA-treated wood, as this will release arsenic into your immediate atmosphere. Instead, take it to your local recycling centre for safer disposal.

538   **Breath of fresh air** Try to watch a few hours' less TV each week, and spend the time you gain enjoying being outdoors engaged in carbon-neutral leisure activities – out and about with friends or family, pottering around in the garden, or simply sitting in the shade of a tree with your nose buried in a good book.

539   **Festive sparkle** Making trimmings for Christmas and other special occasions – particularly with children to help – is so much fun that once you've tried it you'll never buy another decoration again. For example, you can **make tree decorations from a stiff dough (540)** of flour, water and a little salt. Use biscuit cutters to form the shape (or design your own), then bake them in a hot oven until they're hard. Remember to make a little hole in the top to loop string or ribbon through. Adorn your decorations with paints, seeds, glitter or feathers. Packed away carefully after Christmas these treasures should last decades. Shapes cut from felt also make great hanging decorations, and you can **fashion magnificent paper chains (541)** from colourful magazines and old wrapping paper.

Deck your home in a drift of dancing snowflakes (542) by cutting out circular pieces of (recycled) white paper, then folding each one in half three times and cutting v-shaped nicks into the edges of the triangle you've made. Unfold it and thread a loop of cotton through one of the perforations. Depending on their size, you can use these flakes to decorate your tree or hang them from the ceiling, where they'll dance in the breeze. Like the real thing, every one you make will be unique.

543 Virtual faxing Use your computer to send and receive faxes rather than sending hard copies. That way the recipient can decide whether they really need to print out your message or just read it on their screen.

544   **Re-release an album** Impress a music-loving friend by giving them a decorative bowl made from a recycled vinyl record. Vinyl is the second most commonly produced plastic in the world and desperately needs a retirement home.

545   **Trash mob** Give some "tender, loving care" to a rubbish-strewn green space in your neighbourhood by organizing a litter blitz with some friends or neighbours. Divide the litter into recyclable categories and bin the rest. Then take off your gloves, wash your hands and have a picnic in your newly reclaimed green area (don't forget to pick up your wrappers!).

546   **Meter your flow** Most households find that having a water meter, and therefore being charged according to the amount of water they use, reduces their water bills as they become more conscious about avoiding wastage. If your home hasn't already got a meter, ask your water company to install one.

547   **Switch off while you soap up** It's all too easy to lose track of time when you're in the shower (whether or not you're singing). To save water, turn off the shower once you're wet, lather up with soap and shampoo at your leisure, and switch the flow back on only once you're ready to rinse off. Note: this can be unpleasant in a chilly bathroom, so keep the window closed!

548   **Idling time** Turn off your engine if you're going to be stationary for more than two minutes. You'll save fuel and avoid unnecessary wear to cylinders, spark plugs and the exhaust system.

549   **Overload** The more work you ask your car to do, the more fuel it'll use. So make sure it's not lugging unnecessary weight around by clearing out the boot regularly.

550   **Be a survivor** Live lightly, learn some bushcraft skills and discover how possible it is to look after yourself, work with the land, and live happily with less (see page 372).

551   **Happy wrapper** Look for unbleached greaseproof paper. This has none of the chemical compounds often to be found in bleached greaseproof paper. After use, you can scrunch up the sandwich-smeared paper to provide valuable fibre for your compost heap.

552 **MICRO-GARDENING** You don't need a garden to develop green fingers – you can grow herbs on your kitchen windowsill, salads in window boxes, tomatoes in grow-bags and potatoes in a stack of old tyres filled with compost (see page 114).

553 **Wear the right jeans for the job** If you're working hard on a home-improvement or gardening challenge, kit yourself out with some super-durable hemp jeans. Hemp fibre is about three times stronger than cotton, as well as having unimpeachable environmental credentials (see page 109).

554 **Shop at the dump** Before you go on a spending spree at the builder's merchants or furniture shop, see what bargains are available at your local dump or recycling centre. Many sell items such as timber and furniture for small change. Perfect material for DIY projects.

555 **Inspiration and aspiration** Ecological design and architecture used to suffer from a worthy and frankly often downright unattractive image. But all that's changing as a new generation of designers and contractors take on the challenge of making gorgeously eco-friendly places that even the most discerning among us would aspire to live in. Marvel at the inspirational creations featured on eco-building TV shows, such as *Building Green* in the USA.

556 **Make a butterfly box** Many beautiful varieties of butterfly are under threat as human activity encroaches upon their habitats. You can help to reverse this trend. Cut large windows in the sides of a lidded cardboard box, and cover them with fine black netting. Collect plants or weeds, such as nettles, that have caterpillars on them. Put the stalks in a jam jar of water, place in the box, and provide new plants as the old ones are eaten by the caterpillars. Protected from birds, the caterpillars will turn into pupae and emerge as butterflies to be released into the wild.

557 **Ask not to be embalmed** Now that we have refrigerated mortuaries, there's no need for embalming fluids to preserve bodies before burial or cremation. So make sure your relatives know you'd rather skip this toxin-heavy process.

558 **Give your windows a treat** Curtains and other window dressings can make a real difference to the way a room looks, as well as keeping your home cosy in winter and blocking out unwanted heat in summer. Since they're subjected to limited wear and tear, quality second-hand curtains are often an excellent buy – there are even businesses that specialize in this area.

559 **Pets don't need TV dinners!** Avoid single-serving pouches of dog and cat food. These imitations of human ready meals are a waste of money and packaging. Buy your petfood in bulk, and save these dainty sachets for very occasional pet meals away from home, if you buy them at all.

560 **Don't pick on small fry** When you're choosing fish, avoid buying undersize or immature ones. The younger they are, the less likely they are to have had a chance to breed before being caught, so the greater the impact of your meal on the depletion of fish stocks.

561 **How can we improve your stay?** If you're staying at a hotel, motel or bed and breakfast that doesn't seem to have paid much attention to saving energy and resources, give the management some ideas about how they could pep up their environmental performance (see page 373).

562 **Pass on unwanted footwear** Charities are always grateful to accept lightly worn shoes that you've grown out of or got bored with for sale in their shops or for delivery to needy recipients. So clear out that dusty shoe graveyard under your bed and send your unloved footwear packing.

563 **Take them to the cleaners** If you've got a dry cleaning or professional laundry habit, you've also probably got a huge colony of wire coathangers breeding in your wardrobe. Why not take them back to the cleaners with your next load of laundry for them to reuse?

564 **Liberate yourself from the laundry** Despite what soap powder ads might lead us to believe, most clothes don't need washing after every wearing. That's not to say that you should wait until they can walk to the washing machine by themselves, but don't launder them before they're actually dirty.

There are several tricks you can use to keep clothes fresh. For example, **put away "clean enough" clothes right after wearing (565)** to stop them from mixing with the truly unwearable stuff. If they're only slightly crumpled or stale,

**hang already-worn garments outside or by a window to
air (566)**, or in the bathroom while you take a shower to steam
out light creases.

Apart from benefiting the environment, washing and drying
clothes less often keeps them looking newer for longer. And with
less laundry to do, you'll have more time and money for the
activities you actually enjoy.

---

567 **TURN YOUR SHOES INTO A FOOTBALL FIELD**
When your shoes are beyond resuscitation
by even the most skilled cobbler, make sure
they're recycled rather than sent to landfill.
The rubber in their soles has a multitude of
uses – for example, as an ingredient of the
"turf" for all-weather sports pitches.

---

568 **Look for the blue tick** Take the guesswork out of ethical
fish-buying by looking for fish products carrying a symbol that
incorporates a blue tick into the outline of a fish. This shows that
the fish has been certified as coming from a sustainable source
by the Marine Stewardship Council (MSC).

569 **Fruitful activity** Get your children involved in cultivating some fruit and vegetables from scratch. Grow strawberries in pots, plant a few gooseberry bushes (watch out for the thorns!) or sow a couple of rows of carrot seeds. If you haven't got space to grow your own, **go on an outing to a "pick-your-own" fruit farm (570)**.

571 **Water funnel** Use an upturned plastic bottle with the bottom chopped off and the neck buried in the ground to channel water directly to plants' and trees' roots, where it's really needed. Otherwise, during dry spells, any water's likely to run off the surface of the soil so that little gets to your plants.

572 **Take yourself off the menu** Keep biting insects at bay with organic, chemical-free, herbal-based repellents. Most conventional insect repellents contain a pesticide called DEET, which can have many nasty side effects – ranging from rashes to convulsions – and is bad for the environment. Natural options are readily available, work just as well and smell better.

573 **Cistern alert** Put a few drops of food colouring into your toilet cistern. If it seeps into the bowl, you have a leak. Fixing it will be easy, and can save more than a thousand litres of water a month.

574 **Caviar caveat** It may not cross your path often, but when it does, turn your nose up at beluga caviar. The market in sturgeon eggs has reduced the number of these fish in the Caspian Sea by 90 per cent in the last 30 years, and the entire population is under such threat that some countries have now banned imports of beluga in an attempt to save the species. You'll be pleased to know there are sustainable options – **look for onuga "caviar" (575)** from the more plentiful herring. And wash it down with some biodynamic champagne (see pages 202–203)!

576 **Don't stick with non-stick** Use stainless steel saucepans or iron-bottom cookware instead of non-stick pans. Over-heated non-stick surfaces release fumes that kill birds like canaries very quickly – which doesn't bode well for the inhabitants (feathered or otherwise) of your kitchen.

577 **Junk faxes** Stop your home or work fax machine churning through paper unnecessarily (and annoying you incessantly) by barring unsolicited faxes. Contact your national mail/fax preference service (see page 373) to have your fax number made unavailable to unsolicited callers.

578 **Rake's progress** Rake up dead leaves instead of using a leaf blower – you'll save energy, get strong arms and avoid annoying the neighbours. If you really need a power tool for a hard-to-reach spot like the roof, **use an electric leaf blower rather than a petrol-powered one (579)**. They're usually quieter and more energy-efficient. However you gather your leaves, make them into leaf mould (see pages 250–251) to feed your garden, rather than just throwing them away.

580 **RELEASE YOUR BOOKS INTO THE WILD** Once you've read a book, leave it lying on a park bench, or in some other public place, with a note inside inviting whoever finds it to take it, read it, then re-release it. If you also write in an ID number, available by registering your book at www.bookcrossing.com, you can track it as it changes hands.

581 **Pens and pencils** Stock up on pens and markers that contain non-toxic ink, and crayons made from soybean oil instead of more harmful chemicals. And **look for pens and pencils made from recycled materials (582).** Many attractive and effective writing implements are now made from plastic, newspapers, fabrics and even money. For maximum effect, ask your employer to supply them in your workplace.

583 **Stop wasting wine without getting wasted** Much as you might like to use the "waste not, want not" principle as a pretext for overindulgence, you don't have to finish a bottle of wine in one sitting to stop leftover wine going sour. The key to keeping wine for another occasion is to stop it becoming exposed to oxygen. Using an inexpensive vacuum pump to remove the air from the bottle and stoppering it with a reusable rubber "cork", the wine will stay fresh for several days. You'll cut back on headaches and create fewer empty bottles to recycle.

584 **Eco-friendly tippling** Biodynamic wine is the product of a holistic process of organic agriculture that works with the rhythms of nature. Planting and harvesting take place with an eye to the phases of the moon, and the soil is viewed not simply as a growth medium for the grapes, but as an organism in its own right. While this ethos may sound far out, biodynamic wine has the very real benefit of being free from harmful fumigants, insecticides, fungicides and herbicides. Studies show that biodynamic farms have more organic matter and microbial activity in their soil than conventional counterparts. And anecdotal evidence suggests that biodynamic wine drinkers are among the Earth's happiest creatures!

585 **Grass-free gardening** If you're looking for a way to cut down on the amount of mowing and watering your garden needs, you could try replacing your lawn with some alternative ground cover, such as yarrow, thyme, alyssum, sweet woodruff or periwinkle. Ask a local nursery which plants would best tolerate your local growing conditions.

586 **Concentrate!** Try to buy concentrated products (such as washing-up liquid) whenever possible. That way you won't be paying over the odds for products heavy with water that you can easily add yourself.

587 **Make some feathered friends** Nesting sites can be at a premium, particularly in urban areas. Put up some bird boxes around your garden and watch (from a discreet distance) the residents' families grow in their secure new homes. Remember to clean them out at the end of each breeding season to reduce the risk of spreading parasites or infection.

Having given them shelter, make sure that you also **feed the birds in your garden (588)** – particularly through the winter. Stock up your supplies regularly and reliably with a range of suitable foods (see page 370). For a special treat, **make a fat ball (589)**: melt some suet or lard (vegetable oils aren't suitable) and stir in nuts, seeds and raisins, pour the mixture into a small bowl and part-submerge a piece of string in it. Put the bowl in the fridge to solidify, then remove the ball and tie it to a branch with the string.

590 **Leave your lawnmowings on the lawn** Rather than throwing them away and then covering your hallowed turf with fertilizers, let grass clippings rot into the lawn, where they'll release nutrients back into the soil. Just make sure you mow when the grass is dry, so that the cuttings don't clump, which can stifle new growth.

591 **Make your fish go further** If you want to keep fish in your diet, choose carefully, and make sure you don't waste a single bit of these precious creatures. Use the heads and bones to make stock for fish stews, pies or soups and give the skins to a grateful pet cat or dog.

592 **NOBLE ROT** Rotting wood is a common feature of wild ecosystems. It recycles nutrients back into the soil and provides a habitat for a wide range of creatures – as you'll know if you've ever peered underneath a decaying log. So help things along by leaving a few logs to rot in an unobtrusive part of your garden.

593 **Outflank garden pests** You can now buy batches of natural predators such as ladybirds, predatory mites and lacewings through gardening sites on the internet. These handy creatures can help keep pests at bay without the need for chemical treatments. But be sure to check that they'll eat only the critters you want to get rid of, or you could upset the natural balance of your garden.

594 **Horticultural viagra** To boost your garden's fertility, try adding bone meal, wood ash or stone meal to your natural compost. These natural substances won't leach nitrates into groundwater, so you'll avoid contributing to the distortion of aquatic ecosystems by synthetic fertilizers.

595 **Hoe-down** To ensure that your plants benefit fully from any water you give them, take a moment to lightly hoe the soil around them first. This breaks up any crust that may have formed on the surface of the flower bed, allowing water to penetrate the surface and sink down to the roots, where it's really needed.

596 **Salad savvy** If you're making a salad with hard-boiled eggs, keep the cold water from rinsing the salad leaves to plunge the cooked eggs into to cool them down – and don't forget to keep the nutrient-rich water that you boiled the eggs in for feeding your houseplants or the garden (see page 60)!

597 **Try dye** Look for clothing and other items coloured with subtly beautiful natural dyes. And if you're feeling adventurous, you could even have a go at making your own pigments from roots, nuts, bark or flowers. Choose blossoms that are in full bloom, ripe berries and mature nuts, and remember never to gather more than half the crop of anything growing in the wild so that the plant can regenerate. To make the dye solution, chop the plant material into small pieces and place in a pot. Cover with double the amount of water, bring to the boil, then simmer for about an hour. Strain, then add the fabric to be dyed. For a stronger shade, leave it to soak overnight. Depending on the dye, you may need to pre-soak the fabric in a mordant (fixative) to ensure the colour sets.

598 **Ice your wine** Rather than pouring away leftover wine, drain undrunk glasses into ice cube containers and store in the freezer for the next time you need wine to cook with. No lingering germs will survive the freezing and boiling processes, and you won't need to crack open a fresh bottle for the pot.

599 **Bag your bags** If you buy packaged food, rinse the plastic wrap or bag it came in for reuse. Many types of plastic can be used again and again, so you should never need to buy sandwich bags or cling film to wrap your food.

600 **A good old soak** To save water (and elbow grease), leave pots and pans with stubborn food remains on them to soak for a while before you try to wash them, rather than holding them under running water while you scrape them clean.

601 **Watch and learn** Watch nature documentaries with your children and vicariously enjoy the wonders of the natural world. The BBC has produced some magnificent programmes, such as the *Planet Earth* series, which should inspire even the most Playstation-obsessed youngster.

602 **Lesser of two evils** It's healthiest for your garden to keep it completely free from chemicals. But if you have an exceptional reason to use a chemical treatment – perhaps you've suffered an infestation of a particularly vigorous weed – try to find the most benign one available. Check it's specifically designed for garden use, and apply it in the smallest quantity possible in only the precise area needed. Try to find a product designed to address your particular problem, rather than a broad-spectrum toxin such as atrazine or lindane, which will indiscriminately kill any living organism it touches.

603 **Moth watch** Moths are often overlooked as butterflies' dowdy relatives. But they have a subtle beauty of their own, which you can really appreciate during a nocturnal moth-spotting session. Attract the moths with an outdoor light and hang an old white sheet or cloth beneath it for them to land on. Get up close to observe their beautiful, muted markings and colours. If you have children, let them join in – apart from anything else they'll enjoy staying up late!

604 **The boy on the beach** Ponder the story of a little boy on a beach throwing stranded starfish back into the ocean. "Why do you bother?" a man asked him. "There are hundreds of them. You couldn't possibly save them all." "No," the little boy answered, "but I can save this one, and it makes a difference to him."

605 **Cooler rinse** A washing machine uses up to 90 per cent of its energy heating water. A warm wash and cold rinse will work just as well on nearly all clothes as a hot wash and warm rinse.

606 **Scald your weeds** Rather than using environmentally damaging herbicides or fungicides to keep weeds at bay, try pouring boiling water on them. The plants will shrivel and die, leaving no toxic residues. Just remember to boil only as much water as you need, and be careful not to pour it on your legs!

607   **Cool school uniform** If your children wear uniform to school, chances are it'll be made from artificial fibres that leave your kids hot and sticky, and have unpleasant environmental impacts. Look for Fairtrade, organic-cotton school clothing and **give details of green suppliers to your children's school (608)**.

Children often grow out of their uniform well before it's worn out. So whether or not you manage to find ethically sourced fabrics, **pass on outgrown uniform to younger siblings or other pupils (609)**. And, if it hasn't already done so, **ask your school to set up a second-hand uniform shop (610)** – it's likely that many other parents would be keen to take advantage of such a money-saving scheme.

611   **As if you'd never been there** Camping is a low-impact way to see the world if you take a little care. **Select a site that's already been used (612)**, to avoid encroaching on virgin ground. Be extremely vigilant when making campfires (if allowed), and **always dampen your fireplace afterwards (613)** to ensure it's fully extinguished. Leave as little trace of your presence as possible: **take all your rubbish away with you (614)**. Wash yourself, your dishes and your clothes at least

30 metres away from rivers, streams, lakes or ponds to **avoid polluting water sources (615)**. Use biodegradable soaps and pour washing water onto the ground rather than into streams. That goes for brushing your teeth, too.

616 **Don't con your air con** If you need to use an air conditioning unit, make sure it's not getting the wrong message about the temperature of your room. Placing a heat-generating electrical appliance such as a lamp or TV nearby will fool the thermostat into overdrive, making it blast more cool air into the room than necessary.

617 **A hedge can be a home** If you've got a dilapidated garden fence that needs replacing, consider planting a hedge instead. You won't need to coat it in potentially harmful wood preservative and it will provide food, shelter and maternity facilities to all kinds of wildlife, including sparrows and hedgehogs. To give indigenous creatures a home they can relate to, **choose a species of hedge native to your region (618)**. When it has become established (or if you've already got a mature hedge), go easy with the trimming shears. **Leave pruning back until winter is well and truly over (619)**, so that the hedge provides shelter throughout the coldest months. **Don't trim it again until late summer (620)**, to avoid disturbing nesting birds, and **leave berries to develop (621)** so that there'll be a source of food over winter.

622   **Nurture some nettles** If you have space, let a patch of nettles grow in your garden. They attract butterflies, bind the soil and provide it with a rich source of nutrients. Simply cut them at the base at the end of the summer and leave them to rot into the ground, or add them to your compost heap. While they're still young and tender, you can **harvest nettles to make tea, steam as a delicious vegetable or blend into soups (623)**. Just remember to wear thick gloves when picking them!

624   **Set up a wormery** If you have limited space for composting, a wormery could be the solution. These specially designed, compact compost containers house tiger worms, which eat up to half their own weight in waste every day. You can buy a full kit, complete with worms, or get the worms separately from a fishing or composting supplier. The worms can eat virtually any organic kitchen waste, including peelings, cooked and uncooked scraps and teabags. However, **don't feed them citrus peel, onions or garlic (625)** – the worms don't like them. You'll end up with a top-quality compost, as well as a fertilizing liquid which can be collected from a tap at the bottom of the wormery, diluted 1:10 with water and used as a very effective all-purpose plant feed.

626 **Harness the heat from beneath your feet** You may think of soil as cold and damp, but in fact a few metres below the surface, the ground is warm all year round. This natural heat can be transferred by a geothermal heat pump to warm your home. In this beautifully simple system, fluid flows through a network of pipes buried in the ground, where it absorbs the natural warmth. Once warmed, the liquid is pumped up to a heat condensor where it "gives up" its heat to your central heating system. In the summer the system can be reversed to cool your home. Such systems are becoming de rigueur for any self-respecting new eco-development, and can also be retrofitted into an existing home. They may not be cheap to install, but will save you a packet in heating bills. Satisfied customers include Elton John and Queen Elizabeth II.

627 **Snow limits** If you want to ski or snowboard off-piste, ask your local ski guide for advice about where to go. In some areas, going off-piste can cause severe damage to the natural environment and even increase the risk of avalanches. Always stay within the boundaries of the ski resort, especially where it borders on a national park, heritage site or conservation area.

628 **TURN IT DOWN** Many homes are much warmer than necessary in the winter. Try turning the heating down a touch. You're unlikely to notice the difference in temperature, but every degree Celsius you reduce it by should save about 10 per cent on your heating bill. If you're feeling chilly, **put a jumper on or do some chores (629)** before you turn up the heat. You'll probably find you're more than warm enough.

630 **Don't be clumsy around coral** If you're lucky enough to witness the wonder of a coral reef close up while snorkelling or diving, take great care not to damage it by touching these delicate creatures. Coral reefs are under great threat from human activity – from sediment sludge washed out to sea as a result of deforestation to rising sea temperatures as the climate changes. Don't weaken them further with clumsy limbs or greedy fingers.

631 **Hands off!** Wild flowers look so pretty growing in their natural setting, it can be tempting to try taking some of that beauty home. But wild species tend not to last long when picked, so leave them to flourish in their natural habitat. If you'd like to enjoy some wild floral beauty at home, **sow some open-pollinated "heritage" seeds in your garden (632)**.

633 **Way to go, Kyoto!** Averting global warming and climate change (see page 17) requires concerted action from individuals, organizations and nations worldwide. The Kyoto Protocol, an international treaty requiring its signatories to limit their emissions of greenhouse gases, is a good start. It will limit emissions by only a small fraction of what's needed to get back to steady atmospheric and climatic levels, and a few nations are yet to sign up. But it's setting a precedent for more stringent initiatives, and inspiring action even within countries that haven't ratified the treaty – such as the US, where more than 300 mayors have pledged that their cities will meet the Kyoto targets.

Find out what your government, region or city is doing to limit CO_2 emissions (634), and pledge your support for bigger reductions.

635 **Burnished gold** Clean gold jewellery gently with toothpaste, or a paste of salt, vinegar and flour. Try using an old toothbrush to access all the surfaces of intricate designs.

636 **Green home from home** Needing to look after its guests' every need around the clock, the average hotel guzzles a huge amount of energy. The good news is that more and more hotels are becoming environmentally friendly as interest in green issues grows, and more will convert if there's sufficient demand. Show your support by choosing somewhere to stay from a directory of "green" hotels (see page 373).

637 **Buy fairly traded souvenirs** Rather than bringing home touristy tat from your holidays, seek out fairly traded local products for your friends and family. Most fairly traded souvenirs are exported, but buying them in their country of origin means that the local workers who make them receive a greater share of the profits.

638 **Make a splash** Play in, on and under the water with barely a ripple of ecological impact in a canoe, kayak, raft, sailing boat, windsurfboard or rowing boat, or try snorkelling, swimming or diving. You'll get into real contact with the aquatic environment in a way that's impossible if you're attacking it on emission-spewing jetskis or a motorboat, you'll get some decent exercise, and other people on the beach will be thankful for the peace!

639 **From hairdryer to air dryer** Allowing your hair to dry naturally not only saves you time and money, but is much better for your hair, which is liable to become brittle if subjected to a daily blast of scalp-tinglingly hot air. So save your energy-guzzling hairdryer for occasions when you need an extra-special coiffure or it's simply too cold to go outside with even remotely wet hair.

640 **Skimp on shrimp** Approximately 25 billion kilograms of fish, sharks, and seabirds die each year as "bycatch" – creatures caught accidentally as a result of indiscriminate fishing techniques. Because it uses particularly fine-mesh nets, prawn fishing is one of the worst culprits. For every thousand of us who stop eating prawns, we can save more than 5,000kg of sea life per year. Alternatively, try to **encourage demand for some of the tasty but neglected species in the bycatch (641)**, such as gurnard and witch flounder. Ask your local fishmonger to stock these plentiful fish and try out some new recipes with them.

---

642 **CELEBRATE UGLY VEG** Odd shapes and unusual pigments generally have no impact on the flavour of produce, but by insisting on strict uniformity supermarkets force farmers to waste huge amounts of food, and limit the variety sold. This also cuts the farmers' profit margins, driving them to more intensive methods. Let retailers know you'd be delighted to eat varied veg and funny fruit, and enjoy the diversity in shape, colour and size that nature intended.

643 **Let's look after our fish** Thanks to our insatiable appetite for fish, more than half of the species caught commercially are being fished so aggressively they can't breed fast enough to keep up, and stocks are severely threatened. You can help to protect endangered fish by choosing to **buy species that aren't threatened (644)**, such as trout, types of carp and tilapia. Bear in mind also that a species that's in plentiful supply in one fishery may be endangered in another. Consult a sustainable-seafood website (see page 372) for the latest details. **If you're ordering or buying fish, ask your waiter or fishmonger where it was caught (645)**, and, if they don't know, move your custom to a more knowledgeable supplier.

If you eat fish for health reasons, you could **consider switching to other foods that contain the same nutrients (646)**. For example, flaxseed oil, rapeseed oil and walnuts are good alternative sources of the omega-3 fatty acids to be found in oily fish such as salmon, tuna and mackerel – try preparing yourself a delicious salad topped with chopped walnuts and finished with a flaxseed-oil dressing.

647   **A barrel of laughs** Beer drinkers can save the planet too. Make your trips to the pub less wasteful by drinking draught beer rather than beer in bottles. To minimize beer transportation costs, go for local brews if possible, or, better still, seek out pubs that brew their own beer.

Similarly, when you're organizing a large party, **order beer in kegs or barrels (648)** rather than bottles or cans, and return them to the brewery afterwards. It'll work out much cheaper, and your friends will enjoy the novelty of free beer on tap.

649   **Switch off on holiday** Most holiday destinations take a lot of energy to reach. Make sure that your holiday's carbon footprint (see page 17) isn't made even bigger by remembering to save energy once you've arrived: turn heating or air conditioning off, or at least down unless it's really necessary, and remember to switch off all the lights and appliances in your accommodation when they're not needed.

650 **"Green" tea** Even the humble cuppa can be made more eco-friendly. Your first step should be to buy organic, fairtrade tea. Check that the teabags are made from recycled, unbleached paper. The next suggestion may have some people turning up their noses, but try it – it works! **Use each teabag twice (651):** unless you're a fan of extremely strong tea, this will allow you to get two brews for the price of one. If you're making tea for more than one person, **use a teapot (652)** – you'll need fewer teabags than if you put one in each mug.

Of course, there's no need for teabags at all. Why not **opt for loose-leaf tea instead (653)?** You'll save on paper, processing and financial costs – and there's no more civilized way to enjoy a cup of tea. Whichever method of infusion you go for, remember to **compost your tea leaves (654)**. They're a great source of nutrients, and loose leaves can be spread directly onto the soil around the base of plants if you haven't got a compost heap.

655 **Interactive holidays** It's all too easy to travel the world in search of new experiences, only to end up sealed in a tourist bubble with little real engagement with the place you're visiting or the people who live there. If you're planning a holiday, why not look into the ever-expanding range of community-based tourism projects which bring tourists into contact with local people. Accommodation ranges from roughing it to luxury lodges, and activities include learning to drum or speak a language, snorkelling, kayaking and horse-riding – as well as relaxing!

656 **A biodegradable stick-up** Secure giftwrap with sticky tape made from cellulose. The chlorine-free woodpulp it's made from is better for the environment than PVC or acetate alternatives (although it will pull paint off walls in exactly the same way as the toxic stuff, so don't use it to stick up posters!).

657 **Go on a naturally helpful holiday** If you want to do something constructive with your free time, try volunteering for one of the many conservation projects organized by specialist charities around the world. Organizations such as Earthwatch allow you to work alongside scientists on environmental projects worldwide, so you can interact directly with nature and learn about how best to look after animal and plant life.

658 **Fill the page** Unless your document needs beautiful formatting for a picky reader, use a smaller-than-normal font size, single or 1.5 line spacing (rather than double) and narrow page margins to minimize the number of pages you need to print out.

659 **Filter out wasted paper** Rather than using bleached paper coffee filters, which may contain dioxins and are a very short-lived use of valuable trees, replace the filter in your coffee machine at home or work with a metal-mesh version, which can be reused thousands of times.

660 **Home infusions** Try growing your own herbal tea. Even the smallest windowsill can support a potted mint or chamomile plant. Simply pick a sprig every time you fancy a brew, rinse it and leave to stand in a cup of freshly boiled water for five minutes. Delicious!

661 **Make your own notepad** Rather than using a brand new notebook for taking messages, keep a neat stack of scrap paper cut into quarters (stapled together into a pad if you prefer) next to the phone.

662   **HELP PROTECT THREATENED SPECIES** While the plight of charismatic large creatures such as whales, tigers and pandas has attracted widespread attention, every day between fifty and a hundred lesser-known species of plant, animal and insect become extinct. Help to protect countless unheralded species by restoring natural habitats in your local area and supporting international conservation efforts.

663   **Don't be a greedy angler** If you enjoy fishing, make sure your sport doesn't make too big a dent in fish stocks. **Catch only as much fish as you're going to eat (664)** or, depending on local regulations, catch and release fish – using a barbless hook, to minimize suffering and maximize the chances of survival of the fish you release. If you're fishing somewhere new, consult the local angling association or port authority to **familiarize yourself with local restrictions (665)** on where, when and how you can fish and which species you're allowed to catch.

666   **Unpack your fridge** Make sure it's just you that's chilling out on holiday by emptying your fridge before you go away. Eat up leftovers, and give your neighbours any perishables you can't finish rather than throwing them away. If there are things that will last and you want to keep fresh, turn the power down to chill these few items. Otherwise turn the fridge off completely.

667   **Rules of the game** Contact with the environment is an integral part of many sports. But how much impact is your enjoyment having on the ecosystem it depends on? Is your cricket bat made from sustainable timber? Have any of your yachting friends ever emptied an oil tank on the water? Do mountaineers really leave only footprints on the summits they conquer? Find out whether there's an environmental charter for your favourite sport. If there is, stick to it and urge other participants to do the same. If there isn't, contact your national sporting federation and encourage them to draw up and publicize a code of responsible behaviour.

668 **When in Rome ...** If you're travelling in far-flung places, be sure to sample the local gastronomic specialities. Locally produced food will be fresher and tastier than anything imported and will have caused much less pollution to get to your plate. You've got the rest of your life to eat what you normally have at home.

669 **Put your holiday in responsible hands** If you want to ensure that your holiday has a positive impact on the places you visit, choose a tour operator that has "responsible travel" policy. Such companies should offer a better exchange of culture with local people, demonstrably benefit conservation and guarantee that some of the money you're paying for your holiday goes toward local communities. Some operators donate to a local charity, or fund conservation and community projects in the destination.

670 Kitchen storage solutions Numerous foods come in jars and other containers that can be used over and over again. Large jars with screw lids are ideal for storing larder basics such as pasta, rice and pulses. Smaller containers are perfect for portions of salad, coleslaw or other treats in lunchboxes. Not surprisingly, ice-cream containers are great for holding portions of food to store in the freezer.

671 Celebrate! The world's not such a bad place, despite some of the challenges it may be facing. Don't forget to celebrate the joy of life here and now along the way – in the words of the baseball player Satchel Paige, "work like you don't need the money, love like you've never been hurt, dance like nobody's watching."

672 House-hunting? If you're buying a new home, look for one with good environmental credentials. Many countries now run accreditation schemes for newly built houses, such as the BRE EcoHomes standard in the UK and the LEED Green Building Rating System® in the USA. Choosing a home with a favourable rating gives you a good head start in reducing your household's impact on the planet.

673 **Location, location, location** If you move house, try to find a new home that's close to where you work, shop and play. Being able to meet all your daily needs on foot is a great way to reduce your energy usage and associated emissions, helps you stay fit and makes for great quality of life.

674 **Phosphate worse than death** Many laundry detergents contain phosphates, which soften hard water. Once they've done their job in your washing machine and gone through the sewage works, they can cause problems in waterways. Because algae feed on phosphates, high levels can cause algal blooms, which use up all the oxygen in the water, suffocating plant and animal life. Help to protect rivers and other waterways by choosing phosphate-free detergents and cleaning products.

675 **Don't keep taking the tablets** Instead of individually wrapped tablets of dishwasher or washing powder, choose boxes of loose powder or refillable bottles of concentrated liquid to reduce packaging.

676 **A system that works on paper** Put a box next to each printer in your office for collecting paper that's been used only on one side. Keep it in a neat pile to make paper jams less likely. Encourage your colleagues to use this supply for printing internal and informal documents.

677 **If in doubt, check it out** If you're not sure whether an item can be recycled, don't just toss it in the recycling bin anyway and hope for the best. Non-recyclables in the mix create extra work for recycling centres and can in some cases irredeemably contaminate whole batches of potentially reusable waste. Contact your local authority for guidance, and if they don't deal with the material in question, find out whether another organization does. If the item's totally non-recyclable, try not to buy it again in the future.

678 **Volunteer yourself some time off work** Many organizations allow – or actively encourage – employees to take time off to do voluntary work in the local community. If your employer doesn't run such as scheme, ask whether one can be set up, pointing out the good it would do for the company's public image. As well as deriving satisfaction from giving their time and skills to voluntary bodies, most people find that they learn a lot in the process.

---

679 **COMPLETE SHUTDOWN** Many modern TVs and computer monitors need to be disconnected at the mains in order fully to disable their standby setting. Make this a part of your daily shutdown ritual, and try to keep cables as untangled as possible so that you can easily identify which socket to aim for.

680 **All your own work** Try making a food that you normally buy ready made – enjoy the satisfaction of sharing home-made pâté, bread or cake with your surprised and impressed guests. Ask them all to bring something they've never made before to a party or picnic.

681   **Lead the way** Talk to your children about how your family can reduce its environmental impact. If they've grown up with the idea of conservation as a part of everyday life, they're more likely to want to get involved in (or at least accept) day-to-day activities such as switching off lights and appliances, driving less, and shopping for modestly packaged, recycled items.

682   **Carpet makeover** Just because your carpet's a little shabby or stained or no longer suits your interior colour scheme, there's no need to replace it. Use a restoration service to re-dye or restore your carpet and avoid the far greater expense of buying and fitting a new one.

    Similarly, if your carpet has annoying, unsightly rucks and wrinkles, don't head for the showroom just yet. Instead, **ask an accredited fitter to restretch it (683)**.

684   **Pedal your wares** Send deliveries around town quickly and cleanly using a bicycle courier service. Completely carbon neutral, despatch riders can nip among jammed traffic, making them the swiftest option for urban businesses, as well as helping to improve air quality.

685 **Clear winner** If you have the option, always choose products that come in glass rather than plastic containers. Glass is far less resource-hungry to produce and easier to reuse and recycle than plastic.

686 **Look up phone numbers online** Do you really need a new phone directory each year? If you look up numbers only occasionally, ask your phone company not to deliver a phone book and look up numbers online or over the phone instead. You'll save paper and shelf space, and be guaranteed to get the most up-to-date information.

687 **Artificial fibres are the pits** The body odour caused by clothes made from nylon and polyester is probably the most benign of their environmental impacts. They're made from petrochemicals in a process that uses large amounts of energy, water and synthetic lubricants. What's more, the nitrous oxide released during the manufacture of nylon is a greenhouse gas more than 300 times more potent than carbon dioxide. When discarded (often because they smell so bad), these fabrics are stubbornly non-biodegradable.

Although manufactured from woodpulp, and so biodegradable, **rayon and viscose fabrics should also be avoided (688).** The plantations the timber comes from often displace old-growth forests and subsistence farmers. If this weren't bad enough, the manufacturing process uses hazardous chemicals, including caustic soda and sulphuric acid. So opt for natural fabrics whenever possible.

689 **Exception to the rule** Not all artificial fibres are bad for the environment. Tencel®, the trade name for the generic fibre lyocell, is a sustainable, biodegradable textile made from the natural cellulose found in woodpulp harvested from trees grown on land unsuitable for food crops or grazing. Unlike rayon and viscose, its production process uses non-toxic, recyclable solvents. Tencel® is a versatile fibre, which can be used for clothing, upholstery, sheets and towels.

690 **Anyone for coffee?** Next time you're after a caffeine fix, look for shade-grown coffee. The farms it's grown on support many more bird species and other types of wildlife and require much less fertilizer than full-sun plantations.

691 **HOW TO CARRY AN EGG** Choose cardboard egg boxes: these are usually made from recycled woodpulp, and can themselves be recycled or composted, unlike the plastic and polystyrene alternatives. If you're buying lots of eggs, buy large boxes or flat trays rather than lots of small boxes.

692 **Tick the box** When you give an organization your personal details, you're often asked (usually in very small print) whether they can send you more information or pass your address on to other "selected organizations". Say no – even if part of you enjoys being deluged with torrents of junk mail.

693 **Tread carefully** Places of natural beauty inevitably attract plenty of admirers. While it can be fun to wander at will, heavy footfall can lead to soil erosion and disturb habitats, so stick to established paths to help ensure there's plenty left for the next generation to see.

694 **Be resourceful** In nature there's no such thing as waste – when it's fulfilled one function, every natural material goes on to be useful in another way. With easy access to plentiful goods, we tend to forget that fundamental principle, and we throw away an amazing 80 per cent of manufactured items within six months of buying them. Think laterally – try to find as many uses as possible for everything you buy, and throw things away as a last resort rather than an automatic response.

695 **Put another log on the fire** Burning wood isn't allowed in some urban areas, but elsewhere it can be an excellent low-carbon fuel if used properly. While an open fire is an attractive focal point, it's a very inefficient source of heat. So for anything more than the occasional evening blaze, use a wood-burning stove to heat your home. To keep it operating at its peak, **clean your stove thoroughly (696)** at the start of the heating season and periodically thereafter. Clear webs and other debris from the air-intake duct, inspect the chimney and remove excess ash from the firebox on a regular basis.

As well as the condition of the stove, the type of fuel you use is important. For efficient heat production, **make sure the wood is seasoned (697)**. If necessary, store logs close to the fire for a while to dry them out thoroughly. To minimize transport costs, **use wood from as close by as possible (698)**, and check that the forest it's cut from is managed sustainably.

699 **Send your clobber in advance** Family holidays can require lots of equipment, but you don't necessarily need to travel with all of it in your car. Consider sending particularly bulky items such as bikes, surfboards or tents ahead by train. This will mean that your car uses less fuel, and there'll be more space for teddies, picnics, toffees …

700   **Share a bicycle** Public bike-sharing schemes are springing up across Europe. Cities such as Copenhagen have fleets of bikes that anyone can borrow to ride around town, picking them up and dropping them off at designated points. Some are run using special magnetic cards, and others rely on simple honesty. Take advantage of these schemes next time you visit a city that has one, and enjoy quick, easy and pollution-free sightseeing.

701   **Convert to a cat** Catalytic converters significantly reduce the pollutants emitted in vehicle exhaust gases. They're fitted as standard to new petrol and diesel cars in many countries, but if your vehicle is more than a few years old, it may not have one. Get your local garage to retrofit this gadget.

702   **Pollution solution** When combined with heat and sunlight, car exhaust fumes form photo-chemical smog, which is damaging to the environment and can cause severe breathing difficulties, particularly in asthma sufferers. Help to improve quality of life for everyone on hot, sunny days by leaving your car at home for short journeys and walking or cycling instead. A much better way to enjoy the sunshine than sitting in a traffic jam!

703 **Off-road but on-track** If you need to drive a vehicle on areas where there's no paved road, stick to established tracks to avoid excessive disturbance of plant and animal life, and soil compaction or erosion.

---

704 **A TOAST TO TOASTERS** For regular toast munchers, a toaster's a good investment, as it will use less energy than a grill. However, if your toast habit's very occasional, it's probably not worth buying another brand-new gadget.

---

705 **Start composting at work** What happens to those few sandwiches always sitting, curling at the edges, at the end of office meetings? Whatever the nature of your place of work, it's likely that you and your colleagues amass a fair amount of compostable waste during your working day. In most cases this goes straight into the bin for landfill, ready to produce methane, one of the most potent greenhouse gases. Talk to your office or canteen manager and see whether they can compost this valuable resource – either in on-site composting bins or by means of a local collection scheme. Each kilogram of rejected sandwiches, apple cores and soggy biscuits will make about 300g of compost – perfect fodder for encouraging verdant plants to detox your office air (see page 20)!

706 **Cut your air con down to size** If you really need an air conditioning system, make sure it isn't too big for your needs. Not only do oversized systems waste energy, but they're actually less effective. Air conditioners remove heat and humidity from a room by passing the air over cooling coils. If the unit is too large, it will cool the room quickly, but remove only a portion of the humidity, leaving the air feeling damp and clammy. An appropriately sized unit may take a little longer to cool a room, but it will remove humidity effectively – and use less energy.

707 **Say it with flowers** Write your next invitation, birthday wishes or thank-you note on Grow-a-Note® paper. This beautiful hand-made paper is composed of 25 per cent hemp and 75 per cent recycled woodpulp, infused with wildflower seeds. When your message has been enjoyed by its recipient, a few months in the soil will transform it into a patch of flowers.

708 **Beware the fatal six-pack** A bevvy of beers on the beach may give you fun and pleasure, but they're not such a laugh for the birds, seals, dolphins and other creatures who may become fatally entangled in the plastic six-pack loops often left behind after beach parties and washed out to sea. Plastic doesn't biodegrade, but after long exposure to sunlight breaks down into smaller pieces, which are fatal if eaten by wildlife. So make sure you clear up properly after your beach picnic.

709 **Be slick with your cooking oil** When you've finished frying food, don't pour the cooking oil down the drain. As well as blocking your sink, it can disrupt the water treatment process by forming a surface film, which smothers the pollution-removing bacteria. Instead, pour vegetable oil into a small container. When you've filled the container, **take it to a local restaurant (710)** that subscribes to a licensed waste-oil collection service. Animal fats can be saved to make a fat ball to feed birds (see page 205).

711 **Don't be a guttersnipe** Be careful not to drop any litter into gutters, as the next heavy rainfall will wash it into storm drains. The water that flows through these systems isn't treated, but flows directly into rivers and the sea, where your careless littering could cause all kinds of harm to the environment.

712 **LET A CORNER OF YOUR GARDEN RUN WILD**
Beneficial insects and small creatures such as
frogs and toads love the damp, shady places
created by a pile of logs in long grass, and
these small garden residents will help keep
pests at bay naturally.

---

713 **Yet another use for vinegar** If you've got any white vinegar
left after putting it to work on your kitchen, bathroom, wooden
floors and windows, you can use it as a final rinse to remove
shampoo build-up from your hair and give it body and shine.
Simply rinse your hair with a mixture of one part vinegar to
four parts water.

714 **City slicker** If you live in a town or city, an electric car is a great
way of getting around. Batteries currently have a range of only
about 50–100km, but that's more than enough for most urban
journeys, and the technology's improving all the time. Charged
from your home (ideally renewable) electricity supply, these
vehicles will produce 97 per cent fewer emissions than petrol-
powered equivalents. They'll save you a fortune in fuel bills,

and in some towns and cities (such as London) they're exempt from congestion charges and parking fees.

715   **Give a gift that will grow** The ingredients can be as simple as a terracotta pot, some compost (ideally home made) and a bulb or two. Cheaper than many bouquets, this gift will last for years, with a much lower environmental impact than hothouse flowers, which tend to be doused in chemicals and are often flown across the globe only to wither within days.

716   **Gardeners' gold** Often seen as one of the nuisances of autumn, fallen leaves should be treasured by all gardeners for the rich array of minerals they hold and their superb soil-conditioning properties. Gather every last one as if they were five-pound notes!

Left to their own devices, leaves can take up to two years to decompose, but there are two main ways to accelerate the process. First, **shred the leaves (717)** to help them break down more quickly. You don't need a special shredder to do this: just rake them into a pile on your lawn and run a rotary mower back and forth over them. When you add them to your compost heap, **mix your shredded leaves with some nitrogen-rich** material (718), such as grass cuttings, leafy weeds, uncooked kitchen waste or manure, or a supplement, such as bone meal. This will help activate the "cooking" process.

If you can bear the untidiness, **set aside some of your leaves over winter to shelter pest-eating insects (719)**, such as ladybirds and lacewings. Either put them in an unobtrusive pile in a corner of the patio, or spread them in a thick mulch on a portion of flower bed.

720 **On and off** Lend your support to the growing campaign to ban standby settings on electrical items such as televisions. The energy saved by this simple piece of legislation would comfortably outweigh that expended in arduous journeys from the couch to the TV set to use the on/off button.

721 **Restoration** Fight to save old buildings in your neighbourhood from demolition. They represent a significant ecological investment, and even in a dilapidated state, they can still be restored and given new life using much less energy and resources than it would take to construct a building from scratch.

722 **Evergreen** For many of us, Christmas is over when there are more pine needles on the floor than left on the tree. You can alleviate this sinking feeling by buying a live Christmas tree in a pot, which you can plant in the garden afterwards and maybe bring back indoors next year. **If you can't replant your tree, try to recycle it (723)**. Many local authorities and garden centres will accept trees in January to shred for composting or to help stabilize sand dunes.

724 **Make your turps go further** Whatever type of turpentine or paint thinner you use, get the most out of each litre by using it several times. Simply allow the used thinner to stand in a closed, labelled container until any paint or dirt particles settle at the bottom. Carefully pour off the clear liquid into a clean container and reuse it for your next paint job.

725 **No need for fabric softener** Beyond imparting a heady (usually synthetic) fragrance to your laundry, fabric-softening sheets do little more than reduce fabric's static cling. You can eliminate the need for this extra, potentially toxic, gunk by dampening your hands, then shaking out your clothes as you remove them from the dryer.

If the weather allows it, line-drying gets rid of static, and helps your clothes smell fresh naturally. Alternatively, **put half a cup of white vinegar in the fabric softener tray of your washing machine (726)** before the wash cycle. Among its many uses, vinegar is a natural fabric softener, and – despite what you might expect – won't make your clothes smell of pickles. The only thing to bear in mind is that you mustn't use bleach at the same time, as the mixture could create toxic fumes.

727   **Be a BUDDy** When you're dealing with materials for a DIY project, remember the BUDD rule: *buy* only what you need, *use* up everything you buy, or *donate* leftovers to a neighbour or community organization, and *dispose* of waste responsibly.

728   **Wax works** Use natural waxes to bring your wooden floors and furniture to a beautiful shine. Made from wholesome ingredients such as beeswax and olive, citrus and lavender oils, they have a lovely fragrance that you may find quite addictive.

729 **CHROME FIT FOR A KING** To make your chrome fittings gleam, apply a few drops of white vinegar or organic baby oil with a cloth or sponge, or rub with the shiny side of a piece of aluminium foil.

---

730 **Have faith** Faith-based campaigning has come a long way from its evangelical origins. Many of the major religions now strive for social and political change, and faith leaders play a key role as agents of progress in a wide range of contexts, from the environment to poverty relief. Whatever your religious beliefs, consider joining well-organized and highly motivated faith groups campaigning on issues you believe in.

731 **Food-friendly oven cleaner** You probably wouldn't consider adding commercial cleaning fluids to your cake mixture, so why spray them inside your oven? Avoid exposing your food to any toxic residues by cleaning the inside of your oven with a paste of baking soda and water. Apply an even layer and let it set for an hour, then rub it off, using light pressure with a fine steel wirepad for tough, burnt-on stains.

732 **Café culture** Coffee grounds are full of nutrients, and are particularly good for acid-loving plants, such as camellias and rhododendrons. Add them to your compost heap or just pour them directly onto the garden, where they will also act as an effective mulch. Just remember to let them cool down first or you'll scald your plants!

For a more substantial supply, **ask your local coffee shop for their used grounds (733)**. They'll usually be happy to offload one of their major waste products.

734 **Curb climate scepticism** If you're still sceptical about the realities of global warming, make sure you're properly informed before you make your mind up – the future of the planet could be at stake! The consensus among respected scientists worldwide is that global warming is happening, and that it's happening as a result of human activity raising levels of carbon dioxide in the atmosphere. There is evidence from around the world that climate change is happening now, and happening fast. Almost all the world's mountain glaciers are melting at unprecedented rates. The Himalayan glaciers are among the most affected – a worrying trend given that 40 per cent of the world's population relies on them to provide their water.

735 **Face the truth** Watch Al Gore's film *An Inconvenient Truth* (2006) for more non-partisan, hard-hitting details about global warming. Take any climate-change doubters you know along with you to share your popcorn!

736 **TVs need sleep too** If you're in the habit of falling asleep in front of the TV or while listening to music, set your appliance's sleep timer (if it has one) to switch off after a certain length of time. No performer likes to play to a snoring audience.

737 **Cleaning capsules** Try doing your laundry with enzyme "cleaning capsules". These small plastic capsules use natural enzymes to clean fabrics – a non-toxic alternative to conventional detergents. You simply toss them in with your load of laundry and refill periodically with enzyme liquid.

738 **Rejuvenate your aluminium** Kitchen utensils made from aluminium are liable to discolour, but you can brighten them by cleaning with a paste of cream of tartar and water, then buffing with a soft cloth.

739 **Truly stainless steel** Modern stainless steel fittings and appliances are the pride of many homes, but they don't look so great when they're smeared with fingermarks and spattered with grease. Resist the urge to blast your stainless steel with toxic sprays, and instead wipe it over with a cloth dampened with undiluted white vinegar – just as easy and effective, far cheaper and (needless to say) much better for the environment.

740   **Real linoleum** The term "linoleum" has been co-opted in recent years to apply to artificial vinyl flooring that often contains harmful PVC. However, genuine linoleum is a natural, non-toxic and biodegradable product made from renewable plant-based materials – including linseed oil, which gives it its name. Always go for the real thing.

741   **Tick-tock** Choose a traditional alarm clock, which can be wound up using your own energy, rather than a digital one, which relies on electricity.

742   **Do not disturb** Wild animals are disturbed by humans across the face of the planet. We destroy their homes to grow our food and timber and build our own houses, and poison them with our pollution. So give the poor creatures a rest when you see them in the wild. Watch and enjoy them without creating a fuss. Be particularly quiet around mothers and their young.

743 RE-KNIT A JUMPER Make the most of spare time while travelling, watching TV or relaxing outdoors by knitting yourself some new clothes. This is a satisfying, low-impact pastime that's easier to pick up than to give up. Rather than buying new wool, try unravelling an old jumper and give the yarn a new lease of life.

744 **Shiny, happy shoes** Commercial shoe polishes often contain environmentally damaging ingredients, such as trichloroethylene, methylene chloride and nitrobenzene. Instead, rub leather shoes with olive oil and a few drops of lemon juice using a thick cotton or terry rag, leave for a few minutes and buff to a deep, natural shine with a soft, dry cloth.

745 **Share your skills** If you have a particular skill, it's likely that a charity or environmental organization in your area could benefit from it. Whether you're a tidy typist, an inspiring teacher or a keen gardener, volunteering even a little of your time could help to amplify the efforts of local campaigners.

If you have experience or qualifications in a professional discipline, such as personnel management, law, finance, IT, marketing or PR, you could be of great value as a board member, trustee, treasurer or committee member. Whatever your talent, find out how you can help.

746 **Copper and brass cleaning** To remove tarnish and stains from copper or brass without harsh chemical cleaners, soak a cotton rag in a saucepan of boiling water into which you've mixed a tablespoon of salt and a cup of white vinegar. When the solution has cooled enough to handle but is still hot, rub the wet cloth onto the metal, allow it to cool and wipe clean. For tougher jobs, sprinkle baking soda or lemon juice on the cloth before wiping.

747 What koala bears never tell you Eucalyptus oil is a useful addition to your natural household store cupboard. It's an effective disinfectant and deodorizer, gets rid of stains such as ink and grease, repels certain insects and even attacks rust.

748 Economy wash Save time, energy and money by washing your hands with cool water instead of hot. According to health experts, washing hands with cool water is perfectly adequate for killing any germs that are likely to be present – unless you've been handling raw meat or fish or work in the food services industry, in which case you'll need the heat.

749 Reload your printer Reconditioned toner cartridges are made to international standards and are available from major computer and stationery outlets as well as supermarkets and high-street chains. Buying reconditioned cartridges helps save valuable resources (each laser cartridge that's recycled conserves the equivalent of around a litre of oil), and will cost you less than cartridges made from virgin plastic.

750   **Natural glide** Try using castor or mineral oils to lubricate switches and hinges around the house instead of lubricants containing toxic solvents.

751   **Good enough to eat** If you need to use disposable plates and dishes for a big event, serve food on biodegradable, compostable dishes and flatware made from corn starch, sugar cane, bamboo, or tropical leaves. That way you'll end up with a big pile of worm fodder that will soon be valuable compost rather than a stack of landfill.

752   **Lower-energy printing** If you need to buy a printer for your home or office, try to make it an inkjet model, as these use about a sixth of the energy that laser printers get through. **If you need to buy a laser printer, look for one with an energy-saver feature (753).** This reduces energy use when idle by more than 65 per cent.

754 **Go blank** Computer monitors use approximately 90 watts of power when they're on (even when screensavers are operating), but only a few watts when they're in power save, sleep or hibernate modes. So make sure your workstation isn't gobbling energy unnecessarily when your back's turned by switching your screensaver setting to "none" or "blank screen".

755 **Laundry revolution** You can eliminate chemicals from your laundry routine by using "eco-balls" instead of detergent. These Saturn-shaped spheres contain magnetic pellets, which produce ionized oxygen, enabling the water in your machine to penetrate deep into your washing and draw out dirt, while softening fabrics at the same time. Fans claim that the only things eco-balls won't do that detergent and fabric conditioner can are provide an artificial fragrance for your clothes, irritate your skin, fill up your cupboards and empty your wallet.

756 **Clean and fresh** To get pungent smells such as onion, garlic or fish off utensils and chopping boards, wipe them with vinegar and wash in soapy water.

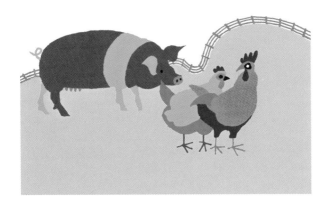

757 **Stuck for gift ideas?** You're not the only one. Apparently, the UK alone spends £1.2 billion each Christmas on unwanted gifts. So instead of another set of scented soaps or pair of novelty socks, give something that will really last. Oxfam, Christian Aid and other charities offer a range of gifts you can give to developing countries on behalf of your loved one – from a goat, pig or chicken to a water purification system. **Sponsorship or adoption of an endangered species (758)** is a great gift for children. Alternatively, **dedicate a tree (759)** or area of forest to someone you love for a gift that will probably outlive them.

760 **ESCAPE FROM THE DAILY GRIND** Kitchen sink waste disposal units need lots of water to operate properly, and add considerably to the volume of solids in septic tanks, which can lead to maintenance problems. Rather than putting your food waste down these revolting contraptions, put it to good use in a compost heap or wormery (see page 215) instead.

---

761 **Police your polystyrene use** Polystyrene is a ubiquitous part of convenience culture, cropping up in everything from disposable coffee cups to fruit wrappers, egg boxes to packing cases. This synthetic material is made from valuable petrochemicals and doesn't biodegrade, so try to use it as little as possible. If, despite your best efforts, you do build up a stockpile, **find out whether any recycling centres in your area accept polystyrene (762)** for recycling. Some do, but most don't – because it's so bulky, transport and processing are prohibitively expensive.

763 **Herbal hair happiness** The secret to healthy hair may lie a few yards away in your garden. You can make your own completely natural hair treatments for free from common herbs and plants. For example, **use lavender or thyme to tackle dandruff or an itchy scalp (764)**: boil four tablespoons of the dried herb in 500ml water for ten minutes, let the decoction cool, then work it into your scalp (having dampened your hair), and leave for an hour before rinsing. **Use rosemary in the same way to stimulate hair growth or condition dark hair (765)**.

766 **Nothing's perfect** Energy-saving compact fluorescent lightbulbs (CFLs) do have one drawback, which is that they contain mercury, a toxic metal that evaporates easily and can travel long distances in the atmosphere, contributing to local, regional and global pollution. This means that it's particularly important not to put CFLs into your general rubbish, because the bulbs would almost certainly break, releasing the mercury. Fortunately, they can be recycled in a controlled process that stops the mercury from escaping. If your local authority doesn't accept expired CFLs for kerbside collection, ask it to do so in the future. Meanwhile, take them to your nearest recycling centre. Bearing in mind how much longer CFLs last than traditional incandescent lightbulbs, this isn't a trip you'll need to make very often.

767 **Give natural bouquets** Flower growing has become one of the planet's most pesticide- and poison-intensive agricultural activities. Many cut flowers are doused with insecticides, fungicides and growth regulators, and fumigated with methyl bromide, which is toxic to humans and depletes the ozone layer. So protect growers, the environment and your lover's nostrils by giving sweetly scented organic Fairtrade flowers. Better still, grow your own, or give a potplant for longer-lasting pleasure.

768   **Outdoor learning** Modern (particularly urban) environments are often devoid of dedicated places for children and young people to explore and enjoy nature. Help to redress the balance by encouraging your local school or community group to develop outdoor learning centres in your neighbourhood or on school grounds. For starters, try creating a discovery trail, butterfly garden, sundial, weather station, acid-rain monitor, bird hide, pond, feely boxes or interpretation materials. Make sure you get the children who'll be using the facilities involved in making them so they end up with something they really like and cherish.

769   **Ethical insurance** Next time you need to take out motor or travel insurance, get a quote from one of the increasing number of providers that pay carbon offsets (see page 373) on your behalf according to the distance you travel.

770   **Careful with your antifreeze** Most antifreeze contains ethylene glycol. This is toxic to start with, and becomes even more so as it picks up toxic substances such as benzene and lead from your car's engine. Keep this lethal mixture tightly sealed in a safe place, as it's deadly to animals and children, who might be attracted by its sweet taste. Never pour used antifreeze into your rubbish bin, down drains or sewers or onto the ground. Instead, take it to a recycling centre or hazardous waste depot, or ask your local service station or car dealer if they can deal with it. **Look for propylene glycol-based antifreeze (771),** which is less toxic than the commonly used ethylene glycol versions.

772   **A word or two about motor oil** Check that you're using the right type of oil for your car's engine: if the oil's too viscous, the engine's moving parts will be meeting more resistance, and therefore using more fuel, than necessary. **Change the oil every 3,000–5,000 miles (773)** for optimum efficiency, ensuring that the old oil is recycled.

When motor oil needs changing, it's not because the oil itself has worn out, but because it has become contaminated with particles that reduce its effectiveness. Used oil can be re-refined, which removes all these contaminants and leaves it as good as new. So, next time your car needs an oil change, **ask for re-refined oil (774)**. Stringent tests have proved that it performs just as well as virgin oil.

775   **Get in gear** If you drive a car with a manual gearbox, the way you handle the gears can have a significant effect on fuel consumption. On the open road it's best to get up to top gear as soon as possible, but without accelerating harder than necessary. However, once you're in top gear, don't stay in it at all costs – letting your engine labour can be just as uneconomical as heavy acceleration, so change down when going uphill or around corners. If you're driving an automatic, ease back slightly on the accelerator once the car gathers momentum to allow the transmission to shift up smoothly.

776   **Check your air filters** Clogged air filters can reduce your car's efficiency, making it use up to 10 per cent more fuel than necessary. So keep the filters clean and replace them regularly.

777 **On the boil** Rethinking the way you cook on the hob can save time and energy. Simple measures include: **putting lids on saucepans (778)** to stop heat escaping; **selecting a pan no bigger than required (779)** for the amount of food you're cooking and a ring no bigger than the pan, and **chopping up food into smaller pieces (780)** so that it cooks more quickly. And get the most out of each ring's energy by doubling or trebling up: **cook several items on top of each other in a stacked steamer (781)**.

782 **Become a Freecycler** The idea behind the international Freecycle movement (see page 371) is simple: members receive for free what they need but don't have that other members have but don't need. This internet-based "free cycle" of goods is facilitated by local volunteers who help turn users' trash into treasure, keeping thousands of useful items out of landfill sites.

783 **Take part in an aquatic clean-up** Find out what local conservation groups are doing to clean up water habitats in your neighbourhood and lend a hand cutting back excess vegetation and removing rubbish from the water and the banks of streams, rivers, ponds and lakes. When the hard work's over, take your friends back for a visit to enjoy your handiwork and watch the area flourish.

784 **Look after your car and it'll look after you** Make sure that you service your car regularly. A poorly tuned engine can use up to 50 per cent more fuel and produce up to 50 per cent more emissions than one in peak condition. Most vehicles manufactured since 1996 are equipped with an "on-board diagnostic system" (OBD), which measures engine function. **Don't ignore your car's "check engine" light (785)**: this is the OBD's way of telling you there's a problem that's causing increased air pollution and reduced fuel economy, so take it to a qualified technician as soon as possible. The sooner you act, the easier (and cheaper) it'll be to repair the fault.

---

786 **CELEBRATE EARTH DAY** Since 1970 each year people around the world have celebrated the planet on 22nd April – Earth Day – through a variety of individual and community activities. Take part in some of the events organized in your area (see page 370), and renew your commitment to help protect our living planet.

---

787 **Be label-conscious** When you're shopping, take time to read the small print. An increasing number of product labels not only list ingredients, but also provide indicators about environmental performance. Look for products that are approved by independent certification schemes, such as the European Eco-label (a small green flower with blue stars as petals) or the US Energy Star, which guarantee that a product has a lower environmental impact than other comparable ones.

788   **Dress to impress** Try making your own mayonnaise. Once you've sampled its fresh, vibrant flavour, you'll be very reluctant to return to preservative-laden commercial varieties. Beat two egg yolks and mix them with three-quarters of a teaspoon of salt, half a teaspoon of mustard powder and four or five teaspoons of lemon juice or white wine vinegar. Then, beat in 250–350ml of olive oil, a drop at a time, making sure that each drop has been absorbed into the mixture before adding any more. To reduce the slim risk of salmonella associated with eating raw eggs, make sure that you use very fresh ones, keep your mayonnaise refrigerated and use it within three days – if you've got any left, you can always put it on your hair (see page 295)!

789   **Out of sight** A tried-and-tested way to satisfy the demands of young children for new toys is to put some of their existing ones away in the attic every so often when they've grown bored with them, and then bring them back out in a few months' time. Your children will greet their new-old playthings like long-lost friends.

790   **Pick your moment** Whenever possible, plan your car journeys for times of the day when there's likely to be little traffic. Not only will you get to your destination more quickly and in a better mood, but you'll save fuel: stop-start driving is less economical than serene progress at a steady speed.

791   **Saving money all the time** By leaving your car at home, you'll of course shell out less on fuel. But now infrequent drivers can also save money on their motor insurance: look for a company that offers a "pay as you drive" policy. The lower your mileage, the lower your premium. The more people who pay their car insurance this way, the better it will be for the environment. When the scheme was piloted by an insurance company in the USA, participating drivers reduced their mileage by an average of 20 per cent.

792 **NO FLY ZONE** Give bottles, cans and other containers a quick rinse before putting them in the recycling bin. This will help to stop them attracting flies both at home and at the recycling station.

793   **Don't let your pool be a water hog** Private swimming pools use a huge – and some would say unjustifiable – amount of water. But if you look after your pool actively and responsibly, you can minimize its environmental impact. **If you've got an outdoor pool, keep it covered (794)** when not in use. This will reduce water loss due to normal evaporation, insulate the water against overnight heat loss, and keep the water cleaner, reducing the need for chemicals and filtration. **Check for leaks by monitoring the water level each day (795).** If it drops by more than normal, you may well have a leak: find it and deal with it as soon as possible. Left unrepaired, a leak causing the water level to drop by just 3cm a day in a 3m-by-10m pool would waste more than 300,000 litres per year. To confirm or allay your suspicions, **conduct a bucket test (796).** Fill a bucket with water and leave it next to the pool (with the cover off) for 24 hours. Mark the water level in both pool and bucket. If, after 24 hours, the water has gone down more in the pool than in the bucket, then you have a leak. (If the level in the bucket has gone down more, then you have a hole in your bucket!)

Another worthwhile water-saving measure is to **fill your pool with rainwater (797)** rather than drinking-quality tap water.

This can be achieved using a simple collection tank and filtration device connected to your roof.

798 **Make sure your birdfood doesn't create catfood**
To make sure any birds using your garden aren't easy prey for feline stalkers, keep bird feeders at least 2m away from dense vegetation, where hunting cats might lurk, and nesting boxes well out of moggies' reach.

799 **Flat battery?** The average lead acid car battery contains 8kg of lead and more than 2 litres of sulphuric acid, which are both dangerous to human health and the environment. So it goes without saying that car batteries should always be reclaimed or recycled. Trade in your old battery when you buy a replacement, or take it to a local salvage yard or recycling centre.

800 **Choose a sparky gas cooker** When you're choosing a new gas stove, look for one with electronic (piezo) ignition, which should use about 40 per cent less gas than a model with a pilot light.

801 **GO FOR A RAMBLE** There are few more pleasant ways of spending a bright, crisp winter's day than rambling through some beautiful countryside. Make sure you're having minimal impact on the environment you're enjoying by leaving your car at home. This way you don't have to walk back to where you parked, but can walk to a more distant destination and get the train or bus home.

---

802 **Organize your generosity** Rather than giving randomly to charities, set up regular direct debits to your favourite causes. This will help you and the charity to plan ahead financially, and should be of extra benefit to charities as they can usually reclaim some tax on money given this way.

803 **Tip-top laptop** If you need to buy a new computer, consider a laptop instead of a desktop, as it will consume up to 90 per cent less energy. Make sure you choose one that can be upgraded and has a long life expectancy, and invest in a robust bag to protect it when you're working on the go.

804 **Freshen up your home** Banish mildew from shower curtains and other damp spots around the house with undiluted white vinegar, applied using a sponge or a spray bottle. Leave as long as possible before rinsing. If you don't like the vinegary smell, open the window or burn some essential oil nearby until the pong's worn off.

805 **Put your hand up** Look for volunteer schemes that enable you to help improve social or environmental conditions overseas. Some require a considerable commitment, such as Voluntary Service Overseas (VSO), which places people with professional skills in teaching, management, social work, health care and IT in posts for two years. If you haven't got that much time to spare, or are unsure whether you have relevant professional expertise, other organizations offer shorter placements, from as little as a week. You should gain fantastic insights into life in different cultures, numerous skills that will be useful in future life, and hopefully have the chance to make a real difference.

If you'd like to help, but have responsibilities at home that prevent you from relocating, **consider joining the UN online volunteering programme (806)**. This network links computer-

savvy volunteers with agencies and projects that
need help with work that can be undertaken over
the internet, such as translation, programming,
and writing business or marketing proposals.

807   **A room with a view** For sparkling windows without
side effects, clean panes inside and out with a mixture of 150ml
of white vinegar to a litre of warm water sprayed with a squirty
bottle. Use a squeegee to remove excess liquid, and buff the
window dry with a soft cloth or newspaper. It often takes a couple
of applications for a completely streak-free finish, as the waxes
in any commercial products you may have used previously take
some time to remove.

808   **Expensive luxury** Using a vehicle's air conditioner can increase
fuel consumption by more than 20 per cent in city driving.
Unless the weather's unbearably hot, use the flow-through
ventilation on your car instead. Opening the windows is another
economical option, but only at speeds below 45mph. Above this
speed, open windows not only inconvenience toupee wearers,
but also cause aerodynamic drag that reduces fuel efficiency.

809 **Strength in numbers** Join forces with those who feel the same way as you about an environmental or social issue by signing – or starting up – a petition, and delivering it to the decision-makers you'd like to influence.

810 **Mole control** Moles can damage a garden by producing unsightly mole hills in the middle of the lawn and by literally undermining plants with their shallow tunnels, which cause roots to dry out. On the plus side, they feed on slugs and their burrowing produces crumbly soil that's great as potting compost.

Conventional methods of control, such as trapping, fumigation and poisoning, are inhumane, environmentally harmful and usually ineffective. Instead, **try a solar-powered mole deterrent (811)**, which emits vibrations through the ground to keep our velvety friends at bay.

812 **Rescue mission** Feel like you're stuck in a concrete desert? Think again. Even the busiest city can be home to a multitude of wildlife. Connect with the nature in your neighbourhood and help it to thrive by giving your time to an urban wildlife rescue organization. You'll be amazed how many unseen habitats there are on your block.

813 **DON'T FEED WILD ANIMALS** It can be very tempting to try to make contact with wild animals by giving them food, but doing so can make them less wary of humans than they perhaps should be, and dependent on them for food – and can adversely affect their health. So, apart from garden birds, which can be safely fed with nuts and seeds (see page 205), don't feed wild animals, and make sure any stored food and rubbish are kept out of reach of potential scavengers.

814 **Going postal** The average household accumulates far more rubber bands than it can use. However, your local postal sorting office will always find them useful for batching mail. Next time you're clearing out your kitchen drawers, give your postman an elastic bonanza.

815 **Low-water shaving** Rather than rinsing your razor under running water, use a few inches of warm water in the basin. This will rinse your razor just as effectively, using far less water.

816 **Expand your Fairtrade repertoire** The range of Fairtrade goods is growing fast – there are more than 1,500 certified products available in the UK alone. This socially equitable method of trading enables producers to meet their basic food, health, housing, social security and education needs. In order to continue growing, the market needs active commitment from consumers. So try to add at least one new Fairtrade item to your shopping basket each month.

817 **Flag drag** If you feel strongly enough about a particular cause to fly a flag, don't attach it to your car. One aerodynamics expert has calculated that a car parading two small flags would create enough drag to burn an extra litre of fuel for each hour that it travelled at an average of 70mph. Make your feelings known with a bumper sticker or fly a flag from your house instead.

818 **Tackle your damp problem** If you've got a problem with damp or humidity in your home or office, try installing a solar-powered dehumidifier. This ingenious device ventilates, warms and dehumidifies buildings using only the power of the sun, and so it has no running costs.

819 **Natural sunscreen** The chemicals in standard sunblock can be absorbed through the skin and expose the body to free radicals, which can increase the risk of cancer, and excess oestrogen, which can disrupt sexual development. Instead, choose sunscreens based on plant-derived ingredients, such as aloe vera, jojoba oil and green tea. They work just as well as mainstream products, but without such potential side effects. Alternatively, to enjoy completely unprocessed sun protection from a plant, **relax under the dappled shade of a tree (820)**. You'll reduce the need for lotions and allow your skin slowly to build up some natural resistance to the sun. **Cover up with a wide-brimmed hat and light shirt (821)** when you need to make forays into bright sunlight, and stay indoors during the hottest part of the day.

822 **Help Nelly the Elephant say goodbye to the circus**
If you want to visit a circus, make sure that the only performers playing the clown are human ones. Humane conditions for circus animals are rare, and in some countries the beasts are taken straight from the wild.

823 **Organic growth** Drawing heavily on nutrients to fuel their rapid development, babies and children are particularly affected by the content of their food. So to give them the best possible start, and protect them from the health risks associated with exposure to pesticide residues, try to feed your children organic food whenever you can – even if the rest of the family is still on the conventional stuff.

824   **Nest in peace** Birds are threatened by habitat destruction worldwide, and populations of more than a third of European species are decreasing. If you're lucky enough to have birds nesting in your garden, take care not to disturb them, and never remove eggs from nests – the mother may well be nearby, but is likely to abandon her eggs if they've been touched.

---

825   **KEEP YOUR PAWS OFF** However cute the wild animal you're admiring, you should never try to touch it. You could be carrying diseases to which it isn't immune, and it could return the favour – along with a scratch, bite or sting.

---

826   **Trojan horse** Don't bring plants or animals home from your holidays. Releasing non-native species into the environment can be disastrous, as they may carry disease or dominate local species.

827   **Keep your copper** Copper is 100 per cent recyclable in an efficient process that requires only 15 per cent of the total energy consumed in mining, milling, smelting and refining the virgin metal. So it's worth taking any old copper items, such as wires or piping, to a recycling centre. (Copper alloys, such as bronze and brass, can also be recycled efficiently.) You may even be paid for your contribution.

828 **Avoid canine chaos** If you're visiting wildlife habitats with your dog, keep it close to you – on a lead if necessary – to ensure it doesn't disturb birds and other creatures. Even if your dog doesn't kill them, it may disturb their feeding or nesting sites.

829 **Run!** Running is a free, carbon-neutral way of getting fit. All you need is a pair of running shoes, so get out there and enjoy the great outdoors. If you need some extra motivation, **enter an organized race and collect sponsorship for a charity you admire (830)**. Start off with a local fun run, and if you enjoy it you may just find yourself in a marathon in years to come. Just remember to recycle your trainers when they wear out.

831 **Keep your recycling dry** To avoid moisture contamination and mould build-up, try to keep your recycling dry until it's collected or you take it to the local recycling depot. If you don't have space indoors, try to cover containers kept outside.

832 **Om comforts** Practise yoga on a mat made from a natural, organic and recyclable material such as rubber, cotton or hemp. They absorb your sweat, don't slip, and can be cleaned and washed easily. They're a much better option than the vast majority of today's yoga mats, which contain PVC. This is considered to be the most toxic of all plastics – just what you want to avoid when you're realigning yourself physically, spiritually and mentally to look after yourself and the planet.

833   **Daily discoveries** Help your children's connection with nature to flourish rather than wither by introducing them to a different nature-based activity every day. If you're running out of ideas, try looking at a book of nature games and activities tailored to the seasons for inspiration (see page 368).

834   **Take your children camping** Eating, sleeping and generally having fun in close contact with the natural world can help to build a lifelong love of, and respect for, nature. Take advantage of good weather to empower your child with a sense of self-sufficiency and a love of the earth. Replace the usual distractions, such as toys, mobile phones, CD players and magazines, with binoculars, identification books, whittling knives, compasses and magnifying glasses, so that your children are well armed to interact with whatever they discover. If you're feeling extra adventurous (and the weather's set fair), **make your own shelter out of whatever natural materials you can find (835)**, and spend a night sleeping in its protection. You may want to take a waterproof sheet with you just in case …

836   Sorted! Make your good recycling intentions easy to stick to by devising a simple system for sorting and storing your waste. Find out what materials your local recycling centre or doorstep collection service accepts, and set up a corresponding storage bin system in your home. Have a labelled container for each category of waste in your kitchen so that putting things into them is as quick and easy as putting them into a mixed rubbish bin. Bins with built-in dividers are now available in lots of shapes and sizes – either free-standing or incorporated into your kitchen unit – so your kitchen needn't be crammed with a whole line of new containers.

837   Time is money Whether your roof needs tiling, your lawn mowing, your shopping collecting, your curtains replacing or your furniture restoring, find out whether there's a Local Exchange Trading System (LETS) in your area that could help (see page 371). These schemes run a money-free local economy where people offer their time, skills or goods in return for something of use to them. As well as giving members access to services that may otherwise be beyond their financial means, the LETS concept supports local businesses and strengthens community bonds.

838   **Stick to your list** Before you leave home, make a shopping list of all the things you need to buy. Ideally, keep one on the kitchen wall so you can add things as you run out. This will help you to buy only what you need, and avoid all the impulse purchases we're encouraged to make in large shops and supermarkets.

839   **Feed your follicles** If you're rustling up a batch of home-made mayonnaise (see page 275), make a bit more than you need and use what's left to nourish your hair – it's particularly good for brittle hair. Work in about 100g of mayonnaise while your hair's dry, leave it to set for 15 minutes, then rinse thoroughly and wash as normal. If you're between mayo-making sessions, **try a mixture of mashed avocado and coconut milk (840)** instead, using the same method.

841   **Take your hot water on a short cut** If you're planning a new home or renovation, make sure that your boiler is installed close to where hot water is going to be needed most often. However well insulated your pipes, heat will inevitably be lost as water moves along them, so don't make it travel via too many scenic detours!

842 **DANGLE YOUR DOG A CARROT** Reduce your dog's ecological pawprint by feeding it less meat. Producing meat puts a heavy strain on the environment (see page 30). Unlike cats, which need a certain amount of meat, dogs can thrive on a vegetarian diet. Vegetarian dog food contains all the nutrients needed for canine health, and can be supplemented by scraps (including the occasional piece of meat or bone) from your family meals.

---

843 **Become a TV multi-tasker** Only got one eye on the TV? Use your couch potato interludes as a chance to mend clothes, sharpen knives or even fix your bike. Properly maintained, your possessions will last longer (and with a "productive viewing" policy you may find you limit your junk-viewing hours).

844 **Take a tint hint** Many hair dyes contain harsh chemicals such as peroxide, ammonia, diaminobenzene and p-Phenylenediamine (PPD). Studies indicate that these substances are harmful both to the environment and to humans. The chemicals can enter the skin of the scalp, and regular usage has been linked to cancers of the bladder, blood and lymph. To avoid these nasties, try colouring your hair with natural tints made from henna and other eco-friendly substances. If you feel you really can't live without harsher chemical dyes, at least try to reduce the frequency of applications.

845 **A rose by any other name**
Avoid perfumes and personal-
care products scented with
rosewood or pau rosa,
which are extracted from
the Brazilian rosewood
tree. Over-harvesting of
rosewood (a key ingredient
in some of the world's most famous
perfumes) has almost completely
eliminated this plant from the Amazon.
Instead, look for products scented with
sustainably harvested botanicals or essential oils.

846 **Exert your influence** In the highly competitive
world of retail, companies depend on the value
of their brand and a favourable public
profile. Although it can take time,
manufacturers and retailers
do respond to negative
publicity over their

environmental and social performance. So if you're unhappy about how a particular organization goes about its business, make an effort to join (or start) a campaign for change. The results could be dramatic ...

847   **Cast-iron guarantee** When you're investing in a new saucepan, choose one that will last. Cast iron becomes naturally non-stick with use and is the most durable cookware around, so you'll keep it forever.

848   **Techno-nap** Next time you go for a break at work, give your computer one as well. Set it to enter power-saving mode after five minutes of inactivity. It'll revive almost instantly with the touch of a key when you're back at your desk.

849   **Free-wheeling holiday** Once you've reached your holiday destination, try hiring bicycles instead of the usual rentacar. The rest of your explorations will be carbon-neutral, you'll save some cash for sampling local delights, and have a chance to burn off any you might enjoy to excess!

850 **USE THE SUN'S POWER** Every two minutes the sun gives the Earth more energy than we use in a year. Photovoltaic (PV) technology, which turns solar energy into electricity, is developing at a dazzling rate – global PV energy production has increased by an average of 28 per cent per year since 1993. Make sure your electricity provider is exploiting this infinite resource, and consider supplementing your power supply by installing PV panels on your roof.

851 **Switch it off** Do you need your microwave oven to tell you the time? If not, turn it off at the mains when you're not cooking with it. The average microwave, in active employment for only a tiny fraction of the day, uses more energy to power its digital clock than to heat food.

852 **Living bouquets** Use potted plants in place cut flowers as centrepieces on the tables at any events you stage. You can give them to your guests at the end of the party, or take them home to enjoy for months or even years.

853 **Watch your screenwash** Take care not to spill windscreen-wiper fluid onto the ground or pour it down the drain, as the antifreeze it usually contains is poisonous (see page 270). Except when you need your wipers to cut through ice, home-made fluid made from three parts white vinegar mixed with one part water is an effective non-toxic alternative.

854 **Don't drown your food** Unless you're going to use the cooking water to make soup, to save energy use only enough water to cover the food that you're boiling.

855 **Dispose of smoke detectors smartly** While invaluable in helping to safeguard your home, smoke detectors that work by ionization contain a small amount of radioactive material. They are completely safe unless the chamber in which the material is held is broken. This obviously means that ionization smoke detectors should be disposed of very carefully. When your detector no longer works, return it to the manufacturer or take it to your local waste recycling centre. Alternatively, **install photoelectric smoke detectors (856)**, which don't contain any radioactive material.

857 **Mix and mismatch** The man-made substances contained in cosmetics and toiletries are often tested only individually, and we don't know what effect exposure to a "cocktail" of different products will have on us or the environment. If you use a variety of synthetic cosmetics and toiletries, try to minimize the number you use and avoid mixing them if at all possible.

858 **Use a trailer** If you need to move outsize loads around by car, it's usually better to put them on a trailer rather than a roof-rack (this may not be practicable for certain items, such as ladders). Trailers – particularly lightweight aluminium ones – are more aerodynamic: you'll get through up to 15 per cent less fuel than if you used a roof-rack.

859   **Read between the lines** More and more skin and hair products are being marketed as "organic". But read the label carefully: unlike organic food, organic cosmetics and toiletries aren't rigorously policed. Some manufacturers may be guilty of overstating the eco-friendly credentials of their products, describing them as "organic" even if only a tiny proportion of the ingredients have been produced organically. To avoid being hoodwinked by such "greenwashing" practices, **look for certification by a reputable organization (860)**, such as the Soil Association in the UK or the National Organic Program in the USA. These two bodies allow only products with at least 95 per cent organic ingredients to be certified as "organic".

861   **Don't be a dipstick** If your car drips oil onto the street, the oil washes into storm drains and then into local waterways. A litre of motor oil can contaminate a million litres of water, so make sure you don't contribute to this problem: regularly check your levels and look for leaks under your car. If you do find a leak, get it fixed promptly – and in the meantime **catch the oil with a drip pan (862)** when your vehicle's parked, and dispose of it at a recycling centre.

863 **CHILD'S PLAY** Give your children access to more toys than they could possibly get bored with by joining a local toy library (see page 369). **Donate the toys your kids do own when they're tired of them (864)** to your toy library or, failing that, to local doctors' surgeries, children's wards or charity shops.

865   **Petal power** Replace harsh and astringent skin toners with rose water, which is 100 per cent natural, and has great skin-softening properties. To make your own, steep some rose petals in hot water until their fragrance has infused the liquid. Remove the petals and store the rose water in the fridge, where it will keep for up to a week, or pour it into an ice tray and use straight from the freezer. If that sounds too much like hard work, you can buy rose extract from cookery shops.

866   **A low-carbon future** Radical measures to curb greenhouse gas emissions by rationing individuals' carbon use are being developed by some governments. One plan under consideration involves awarding each of us an identical annual carbon allowance, which could be stored as points, similar to Air Miles® or supermarket loyalty points, on an electronic swipe card. Points would be deducted at point of sale for every purchase closely related to non-renewable energy, such as petrol or air tickets. People who didn't use their full allocation, such as members of families who don't own a car, would be able to sell their surplus points to a central bank. People who exceeded their allocation could then draw the relevant number of carbon points from the bank, with the cost added to their fuel bills. The overall number of points available nationally would steadily decrease each year.

Prepare for the introduction of any such plan by setting yourself a carbon target that's lower than your current carbon footprint (see page 17), and reduce it further next year.

867 **Make your own facepack** Rather than buying fancily packaged facepacks, try making your own from organic, preservative-free ingredients. Mix a teaspoon of runny honey (which is full of vitamins and has antiseptic qualities) with two teaspoons of plain yogurt and a teaspoon of oats. Gently rub the mixture into your face, then leave to dry for 15 minutes before removing with a hot, damp cloth. The yogurt will cleanse your skin, and the oats provide gentle exfoliation. If you've made too much, eat the leftovers!

868 **HARVEST THE RAIN** To cut the amount of tap water your family uses by up to half, consider investing in a rainwater harvesting system. This collects the rain that lands on your roof, and filters it for use in your toilet, washing machine and garden. While still relatively expensive to retrofit, these systems add little to the cost of a new home, and you'll quickly recoup any additional outlay by saving on water bills if your home water supply is metered.

869   **Give your dishwasher a boost** Next time you need to buy a new dishwasher, look for one with a booster heater, which (if necessary) raises the temperature of the water used to wash dishes within the machine itself, whenever you run a wash. This means you can turn down the thermostat on your home's water heater, saving energy and money. Any extra cost of the dishwasher should be recouped by energy savings within a year.

870   **Brown and green** Sunbeds can endanger both your health and that of the planet. Each sunbed contains around 45 energy-hungry tanning lamps, which each hold four times the amount of toxic mercury found in a normal fluorescent tube, causing major disposal problems. Save energy, avoid mercury waste and protect your skin from premature ageing and an increased risk of melanoma by boycotting sunbeds in favour of a natural self-tanning lotion containing plant-derived DHA (the active ingredient in self-tanning products that causes your skin to go brown). Or take the edge off your pallor by applying a natural sunblock and going out in the sun for short periods (see pages 288–289). It's much more pleasant, and you'll top up your body's vitamin D reserves (available from natural light) at the same time.

871   **Coming to a screen near you**
Liquid crystal display (LCD) screens
are currently the most energy-efficient
on the market. But a new contender
could soon join the low-energy viewing
arena: organic light-emitting diodes
(OLEDs) can be used to illuminate
screens using much less energy than
other technologies. Still in their infancy,
OLEDs are currently used only in mobile
phones, but should soon be developed
for use in televisions and computers.

872   **Tidy fridge** Clear out your fridge
regularly to minimize the amount of food
and drink it has to keep cool. By keeping
the fridge tidy you can find what you're
looking for quickly. Up to 30 per cent of
the cool air escapes every time you open
the fridge, so the quicker you can grab
stuff and close the door the better.

873 **Make them work for your vote**
If you're fed up with seeing streetlights left on in daylight or empty public buildings blazing into the night, ask your local politicians to ensure that they're leading by example and show that public facilities are making real efforts to cut their energy use, generate their own renewable energy and generally green up their act.

874 **Simmer down** Unless there are lots of people using it on a regular basis throughout the day, there's no point in leaving your coffee machine's "keep warm" function on for long periods. Turn it off at the plug when you've made your morning cuppa, or it will use enough energy to make 12 more cups before you decide to have another in the late afternoon.

875   **MAKE A POSITIVE DIFFERENCE** "If many little people in many little places do many little deeds, they can change the face of the Earth" (African proverb). Never underestimate the impact of your actions.

---

876   **Need a reminder?** For up-to-date facts and figures on the state of the planet, consult the Worldwatch Institute's *Vital Signs* and *State of the World* reports. They should galvanize you into action!

877 **Healing action** In the 1980s scientists discovered that man-made chemicals were destroying the ozone layer that protects us from the sun's most damaging rays. Governments around the world quickly adopted the Montreal Protocol (1987), which banned ozone-destroying gases such as chlorofluorocarbons (CFCs) – found in aerosol cans, fridges and air conditioners.

Since then, levels of the most critical CFCs have stabilized or declined. There's still a significant ozone hole over Antarctica, but elsewhere the ozone layer seems to be on the mend. This healing may not be attributable solely to the Montreal Protocol, as sunspots, volcanoes and weather also play a role in regulating ozone levels. But it suggests that concerted action to repair our mistakes is possible. If the trend continues, the ozone layer should be restored to 1980 levels by 2070. By then, even the Antarctic ozone hole might have closed – for good.

878 **Visit an eco-village** Communities of people striving to live sustainably are springing up across the world. With any luck, one day they'll be as common as today's suburbs, but in the meantime if you don't know of one near you, contact the growing global eco-village network (see page 372) for information, news, resources, courses and educational programmes.

879   Age of excess "Earlier periods in human history were marked by the material that distinguished the era – the Stone Age and the Bronze Age, for example. Our age is simply the Material Age, an age of excess, whose distinguishing feature is not the use of any material but the sheer volume of materials consumed." (Lester R. Brown, the Worldwatch Institute, in *Eco-Economy*).

880   Write away "The Earth is not dying – it is being killed. And the people who are killing it have names and addresses." (U. Utah Phillips). If you're worried about environmental issues, let your concerns be known in a letter to the people responsible. As well as writing individually, **join a letter-writing campaign (881)**, such as one organized by Global Response (www.globalresponse.org) to help communities stop environmental destruction.

882 **Any colour – so long as it's green** If you need to buy a new car, try to make sure that it's better for the environment than the last one. **Go for a manual gearbox (883)** if possible, as these are 10–15 per cent more fuel-efficient than automatic models. If you don't feel confident driving manually, take a refresher lesson or two to relearn the basics. **Choose the smallest car that will fulfil your regular needs (884)**. For example, do you really need a people carrier if you're the only person in it for most of the year? Might it be more sensible to buy a small car for your daily needs and hire a bigger one for your annual holiday? **Study comparative fuel-consumption data (885)** in order to identify the most efficient model in the size class you want to buy.

If you normally drive a petrol car, **consider switching to diesel (886)**. Diesel engines are 20–40 per cent more economical than petrol engines, and recent models are quieter and emit much lower levels of pollutants than older versions, making this fuel a relatively clean choice. However, for the ultimate in efficiency, you'll need to look beyond the mainstream to new fuel technologies (see page 336).

Whatever car you choose, make a pledge to use it less and share it more!

887 **Relocate a frog family** If you've got a well-appointed garden pond (with plenty of vegetation and sloping sides for easy amphibian access), carefully collect a small amount of frog spawn from a local pond along with a bucket of pond water, and transfer it to your pond to provide a new home for the emerging tadpoles. Make sure that you leave plenty of frog spawn in the place you found it. Cats like hunting frogs, so fit your pet felines with an easy-release bell collar (see page 80).

888 **Stock option** If you have ethical concerns about the way a particular company operates, consider becoming a shareholder. Even if you own just one share, you can attend the company's annual general meeting, where you can raise questions about issues that trouble you. You also have a right to vote on the company's major decisions (although if your stake is tiny, this would have an impact only as part of a wider campaign). Major corporations are increasingly being held to account in this way on issues ranging from environmental destruction to waste disposal, child labour, and sharp sales practice.

889 **Recycled steel's a steal** Look for products made from recycled steel – from paperclips to garden tools and building materials.

890 **Beer can save the planet** Most manufacturing by-products do nothing but harm to the environment. However, in brewing the opposite is the case. Beer bran, a by-product of brewing with barley, can be used to remove pollutants such as benzene from industrial waste, keeping them out of rivers and lakes. So, to support your local ecosystem, support your local brewer.

891 **Catch some rays** As well as appearing on roofs worldwide (see page 300), solar panels are being incorporated into a variety of portable products, thanks to the invention of a discreet, lightweight photovoltaic unit known as the "power pocket". **Kit yourself out with a solar backpack (892)** with built-in power pockets and you'll be able to charge your mobile phone, MP3 player and other micro-devices while you're on the move.

893 **Don't lapse into long-haul** The lure
of the exotic can be hard to resist, but an
intercontinental long-haul flight can produce
more CO_2 emissions per passenger than the
average motorist does in a year – an easy
way of undoing all your good deeds at home. So before you
book a far-flung trip, investigate holiday options closer to home.
You may find far more variety than on an identikit package
further afield.

894 **Cut CO_2 on your doorstep** The average European home is
responsible for emitting 9 tonnes of CO_2 a year. Try to introduce
at least one domestic energy-saving measure each month over
the next year to reduce your home's contribution.

895 **Try mentoring** If you're looking for inspiration about how to live or work differently, try to find a mentor to help you fulfil your potential. If you'd like to give something back, you can make a real difference to someone else's life by becoming a mentor yourself. You'll never stop learning ...

896 **Build with bamboo** Bamboo is often overlooked by builders and designers, but this versatile material is stronger than steel in tension and concrete in compression, and has many uses around the home, from flooring to framing. It's pretty useful while it's growing too, acting as a bioabsorber to clean pollutants out of the soil, preventing erosion and returning more oxygen to the air through photosynthesis than almost any other deciduous plant.

897 LEARN SECRETS FROM THE OLDER GENERATION
Take time to talk to your grandparents or great-grandparents about how they used to live. Experts on doing more with less, they lived without many of the features of modern life that are causing environmental problems today, and may have excellent suggestions for how you could reduce your environmental impact while maintaining a good quality of life.

898 Boil a cuppa using natural fuel
Rather than using a polluting camping gas stove, equip yourself with a storm kettle to provide naturally heated hot drinks when you're out in the wild (or on a dry run in your back garden). Simply feed the kettle with small dry twigs, offcuts of wood or pieces of scrunched-up scrap paper – ideal for picnics and camping trips.

899 **Task lighting** Does the whole room need to be ablaze with light to illuminate you reading a book in one corner? If not, switch off the overhead lighting and snuggle up next to a lamp. If a million homes all reduced their average electricity load by just 60 watts (one incandescent light bulb), they'd cut carbon emissions by around five million tonnes a year.

900 **Energy-free refrigeration** If you don't need to keep many items cool – for example, milk for a small office – try making your own fridge. Take two unglazed terracotta flower pots of different sizes and stack them together with a layer of wet sand between. If you keep the sand wet and cover the top with an old towel or blanket, the interior of the smaller pot should stay cool, as the evaporating water transfers heat energy into the air. You may find you no longer need a conventional electric fridge at all, in which case make sure your old one is recycled properly. If that's too radical a move, keep your energy guzzler unplugged except during the hottest months.

901 **Kick child labour into touch** Worldwide, more than 200 million children under the age of 14 work for a living. Labouring for long hours in poor conditions for minimal pay, these children produce many of the cheap consumer goods that we take for granted. Help to guarantee some of them a better quality of life by looking for Fairtrade items, made by adults who are paid a fair wage, work in good conditions and receive medical care and health insurance.

902 **Turn your boss into a green guru** Faced with the daily stresses of running a business, your chief executive may consider the "greenness" of your workplace a peripheral matter. If so, it's your job to persuade him or her otherwise – not least, by showing them how much they can cut overheads by implementing simple energy-saving measures, such as a computer-shutdown policy.

Rather than putting the onus on your boss to take action, volunteer your own time: **circulate energy-saving tips (903)**, either by "all-staff" e-mail or company message board, and **invite suggestions from your co-workers (904)**. When it becomes clear how much money you've saved your company, it may be not just the environment that benefits, but also your career.

905   **Make your own paper** Put yourself at the business end of recycling: set aside some old newspapers and magazines to make your own paper (see page 372). You can even use leaves from the garden. This is a simple though somewhat messy process that's great fun to do with children and produces uniquely patterned and textured art paper. You'll probably be able to find all the equipment you need in your kitchen, so get pulping!

906 **ANY EXCUSE FOR A PARTY** Why not host a clothes-swapping bash? Ask guests each to bring along a bag of decent-quality clothes they no longer want, keep donations anonymous (as far as possible), agree to ban the taste police, and provide plenty of refreshments to keep people's changing-room stamina fuelled.

907 **Get some advice about ethical investments** If you're not money-minded, thinking through investments can be daunting at the best of times. If finding out about ethical and environmentally positive financial products seems too much like hard work, enlist the help of a specialist financial adviser to help you navigate interest rates and returns that respect your ethical priorities. Alternatively, try an ethical research service website for suggestions (see page 371).

908 **Fund your home ethically** Your home may be the single biggest investment you make in your life. So make sure your financial commitment is achieving the best possible result for the planet by using a green mortgage. These range from light to dark green options. Some of the darker green ones won't lend you money unless your property will give an ecological payback. Other green mortgages provide incentives such as discounts on your mortgage rate when you carry out eco-improvements, planting trees every year to offset the emissions created by your home, or donating money to environmental charities.

909 **Cotton on to organic** Only 2.5 per cent of the world's farmed land is used to produce cotton, but more than a quarter of the world's pesticides are poured onto these crops, making them the most polluting – and polluted – on the planet. So buy organic cotton whenever you can – it's appearing in more and more clothing collections.

910   **Soup your veg** Mixed-vegetable soups, such as minestrone, are a great way to get the most out of leftovers or random vegetables that need using up. Tops of spring onions, celery and cabbage hearts, and tomatoes too ripe for salads can be thrown in. Leftover pasta, potatoes (even mashed), rice and pulses can go in too. If you **freeze leftovers as you go (911)**, there's always something in the house to make a nutritious meal from.

912   **Plan your pulses** Save aluminium and other resources by buying dried lentils and other pulses rather than tinned ones. They're much lighter and less bulky to transport, as well as being much cheaper to buy. **Soak dried pulses for as long as possible (913)** – ideally between 12 and 24 hours – to reduce the time, and therefore energy, needed to cook them. A teaspoon of baking soda in the soaking water can help soften tough skins.

914   **Taming the vending machine** Left to its own devices, the office hot-drinks machine could hardly be described as the greenest of inventions. However, it can be brought into line. For example, **encourage co-workers to fill up with a mug (915)** rather than a disposable plastic cup and provide spare mugs for visitors to use. You could also **ask your office manager to stock the machine with Fairtrade tea, coffee and hot chocolate (916)**. These can now be bought for vending machines and are available at competitive prices.

917   **Drip, drip, drip** Just one leaking tap can waste up to 30 litres of water a week – enough for a good shower. So replace the washer as soon as you hear that tell-tale drip.

918   **Give it a rest** Unless you happen to be a doctor on call or the president of a nation in crisis, remember to switch off your mobile phone before you go to bed. This will save battery power and stop you being woken up at four in the morning by a text message offering you free ringtones.

919   **Give swordfish the chop** Swordfish has been overfished for the past century or more, and stocks are now at the lowest level on record. Most of those on sale are caught before they've had a chance to breed, so depleting stocks further. Forgo this fishy treat in favour of other less threatened species (see page 223).

920 **FROM FIELD TO FORK**
To ensure that your food is
as fresh as possible, buy direct
from the person who produced
it. Shopping in farm shops or
at farmers' markets also guarantees the best
possible return for the farmers, rather than
most of their profits going to supermarkets.

921 **Blankets on the menu** If you're eating al fresco at a restaurant
or café and being roasted by a gas-fired patio heater, ask the staff
to switch it off (check this is OK with other diners). Suggest that
the restaurant get rid of these energy-hungry contraptions and
instead provide blankets for diners to drape over themselves.

922   **Identify your real needs** In an age of abundance, we're barraged with ever-more crazy opportunities to spend money and consume more. Sophisticated marketing is designed to persuade us we need to have more and more stuff in order to be happy. Some luxuries undoubtedly make life pleasant, but many are little more than gimmicks. So when you're tempted to jump on the next gizmo bandwagon, ask yourself whether you really need this latest ecosystem-plundering indulgence. Seventeen million heated toilet seats have already been sold worldwide, and the Japanese manufacturer is hoping to sell 400,000 a year to North America alone. Maybe it's time for a reality check.

923   **Join the real-world gym** A fit body is the ideal vehicle for a healthy, fulfilled life. But staying in shape can seem like one chore too many when your life's already full. Save yourself time and money by opting out of the gym and its energy-hungry exercise machines, and trying some of the following real-world workouts instead.

   Take the stairs (924): you'll get shapely buttocks, while saving the energy required to power the lift. **Walk, run or cycle to work, shops and to see friends (925)**. Tone your arms, shoulders and back: **collect your shower or bath water in a bucket (926)** and carry it out to water the garden, or **chop wood for your fire or biomass boiler (927)**. For a productive weight-training session, **walk your recycling to the nearest collection point (928)** – and if you still yearn for the burn, you could offer to take your neighbours' waste on a separate trip.

929 **Don't get heated up for hot plates** If you're using the oven to cook a meal, you can heat up the plates you're going to eat it from by putting them in the bottom for the last few minutes of cooking – just turn the oven off and use the heat that's collected. But if you're not using the oven to cook, don't waste energy by switching it on just to warm the plates. Instead, place them over the saucepan you're cooking in, and cover with a lid or cloth.

930 **Good tide-ings** The energy held in the oceans' tides, waves, currents and temperature differentials can be tapped for human use. Most such technologies are still at the experimental stage, but several sizeable and successful tidal-power installations are already in place, and Scotland and Australia are among a growing list of countries investing in ocean-energy technologies.

931   **TAKE TO THE HIGH SEAS** If your appetite for long-distance travel won't subside, rather than going on several short holidays by plane, try saving up your leave and going on a longer, potentially more rewarding trip by boat. You can even **travel by cargo ship (932)**, which will be cheaper than a cruise, take you to places the average tourist never sees, and dramatically slash your journey's carbon emissions.

933 **Home brew** If you're partial to a brew or two, spare the environment the cost of manufacturing, transporting and disposing of hundreds of beer cans and bottles by treating yourself to your own home-made organic beer at a fraction of the cost of commercial brands. You can buy a full brewing kit for less than £100 – the only thing you need to provide after that is water. Once you get the hang of it, you'll soon be experimenting with different techniques and ingredients – and it's a perfect excuse for a tasting party ...

934 **The wheel of the year** Phenology is the recording and study of annually recurring natural events, such as the first sightings of species of migratory birds or the first ripening of wild fruit. Climatologists and ecologists find such data invaluable in monitoring climate change year on year and region by region. Every one of us can help in the gathering of this information by taking time to notice and report seasonal phenomena near our homes to a national phenological survey (see page 370).

935 **Clean set of wheels** If you're buying a new car, there has never been a better choice of mainstream alternatives to conventional petrol- or diesel-fuelled models. Consider, for example, petrol-electric hybrids, which can travel 55 miles or more on a gallon of petrol. You can probably even **convert your existing car to run on cleaner fuel (936)**, such as LPG (liquefied petroleum gas) or biofuel, often made from vegetable oil. Biofuel is carbon-neutral, as the carbon dioxide emitted in its combustion is offset by the growth of new crops planted for its production.

937 **Say no to GMOs** Genetically modified organisms (GMOs) have had their genetic makeup altered in a way that doesn't occur through normal breeding or hybridization, in order to give them particular characteristics, such as disease immunity or resistance to pests or drought. Not all the risks associated with these methods have yet become clear, but it seems that the impacts on human and environmental health could be very high. Most of the GM crops currently grown are bred either to resist a herbicide or pesticide – leading to huge increases in agrochemical use – or to produce their own insecticide, which you then eat. To avoid these products, look for food labelled GM-free (see pages 360–361), buy certified organic produce (which can't contain GMOs), and let suppliers know that you're not happy about their stocking genetically modified food.

938 **Walnut wonders** Conceal scratches in wooden furniture with the oil from crushed walnuts. It won't look as pristine as a professional French polish, but will add to the character of pieces that bear the brunt of a busy life.

939 **Self-preservation** To avoid the potentially detrimental impact of synthetic preservatives such as parabens (see page 56) in your toiletries and cosmetics, choose self-preserving organic products such as moisturizing body oils made from cocoa butter or sunflower, peppermint, coconut or spearmint oils. They last naturally for up to 18 months.

940 **SPA TREATMENT** As well as feeding the birds in your garden (see page 205), remember that they also need water – both for drinking and bathing. Get a bird bath and keep it topped up with clean water – preferably rainwater from a water butt. It's best to change the water daily and give the bottom of the bath a quick rinse to prevent the spread of disease.

941 **Say goodbye to pre-washing** Modern washing machines are so efficient that the pre-wash cycle is generally unnecessary. If your clothes are really dirty, leave them to soak for a while before putting them in the machine. Avoiding the pre-wash setting will cut each load's energy use by 15 per cent.

942   **Have a smaller family** This is a difficult subject to broach, but population growth is one of the biggest challenges to achieving sustainability. Over the last century the human population has grown from one to six billion (while life expectancy has doubled), and it isn't expected to stabilize until about 2100, when there'll be about 11 billion people on the planet. Meanwhile, every year each of us consumes more of the world's resources and produces more waste. Since 1972 we've been using the planet's resources at a rate faster than it can replenish them, and most (86 per cent) of that bounty supports the lifestyle of the richest 20 per cent of the population. If the developing world follows our example of how to live, the planet will face even bigger challenges. So while we each work on reducing our environmental impact, it would help if we had fewer children, perhaps adopting more often. If, over the next 50 years, each family had only one child, the population would return to six billion by 2050.

943   **Get your kids gardening** However many children you have, the garden is a great place for them to interact with nature in a meaningful and rewarding way from an early age. They'll quickly learn what plants and creatures need to thrive (and that they don't need so-called "miracle" pesticides and fertilizers), and will gain a great sense of achievement from watching the things they tend grow and flourish – and maybe even provide them with some meals and snacks. If possible, **give your children their own patch of garden to tend (944)** – a raised bed, some containers, a ground plot, or even a disused sandpit. Set them up for success by making sure that their area's right in the middle of the action, with the best soil and light, and giving them proper gardening tools – scaled down, if necessary. Let them choose what they want to do with their plot, but gently **steer them toward crops that are relatively easy to grow (945)**, have short growing seasons and are fun to harvest, such as radishes, cherry tomatoes, sunflowers, sugarsnap peas, carrots and pumpkins.

341

946 **Fly the flag for clean beaches** When you're planning a daytrip or holiday to the beach, look for one awarded a Blue Flag (in Europe) or a Blue Wave (in the USA) for good water-quality management. Support from tourists will encourage accredited beaches to maintain their standards, and may persuade managers of unaffiliated ones to clean up their act.

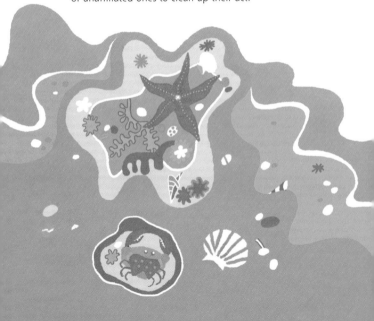

947   **Shade your home with some leafy vines** If you live in a hot climate, shading is the simplest, most effective way to cool your home and reduce energy consumption. Train quick-growing vines up trellises on the hottest side of the house to provide an attractive source of shading and cooling. Make sure the trellis is kept at least 15cm from the building to protect the wall and provide a buffer of cool air. If there's no open soil around your home, climbing plants such as deciduous clematis and wisteria grow well in containers. Ask your local nursery which plants are best suited to your climate and needs.

948 **Summer sleeping** Hot air rises, so if your bedroom's stuffy in hot weather, try sleeping downstairs (if your home has more than one storey), rather than using air conditioning or a fan. Failing that, **create a cooling evening breeze (949)** by opening a window in your bedroom and another in an adjoining room.

950 **FORGO A FANCY FRIDGE** When choosing a new fridge, remember that the simpler the model, the better for the environment. Avoiding snazzy extras like auto defrost, ice makers, and heaters to control condensation can cut the fridge's energy use and running costs by up to 60 per cent, and should also make it cheaper.

951 **Cook a solar meal** For zero-impact cooking, try making a meal in a solar oven (if the sun's out). These portable devices are probably the most energy-efficient cooking appliances available, as they require no fuel of any kind to cook, yet allow you to bake, boil or steam food in about the same time it would take on a normal stove. They're ideal for picnics or camping trips – particularly in areas where fires are prohibited. In fact, there's no reason why you shouldn't turn your garden into a carbon-neutral outdoor kitchen throughout the summer! For rainy days or cooking at night, hybrid versions with an energy-efficient electric back-up are also available.

952 **Little wonders** LEDs (light-emitting diodes) are small, solid, extremely energy-efficient light bulbs. Until recently, they were available only in single-bulb applications, often on electronic gadgets, but they're now available in a variety of guises. They last ten times as long as compact fluorescents, and a massive 130 times longer than typical incandescent bulbs, and use a fraction of the wattage. Look out for LED products such as torches, Christmas lights (see page 148), headlamps and srnall task lights.

953 **Ink stink** Use water-based markers rather than permanent solvent-based versions to avoid exposing yourself and those around you to harmful substances such as toluene, xylene and ethanol. You'll have fewer headaches in the office, and much less risk of ruining your shirt if one leaks!

954 **Look for EcoSpun clothes** Next time you need a durable item of clothing, look for EcoSpun, a high-quality polyester fibre made from recycled plastic drink bottles. It's used to make fabrics such as fleece, and can be blended with other fibres, such as wool, cotton and Tencel®, for clothing as well as carpets and home furnishings.

955 **Fair reward** If you've got a sweet tooth, reward yourself for your efforts to live a sustainable lifestyle by enjoying a bar of Fairtrade (and ideally organic) chocolate. As well as offering a better deal to its producers, Fairtrade cocoa is one of the most environmentally friendly tropical crops.

956 **Accidents will happen** Banish stains from rugs and upholstery using a splash of soda water or a mixture of equal parts water and white vinegar. Sponge the offending mark off as soon as possible after it has formed.

957 **Refreshing break** Rather than going away on a far-flung expedition, why not use your next break to really explore your local area? It's amazing how much more you appreciate your surroundings when you take the time to get to know them.

958   **THE MORNING AFTER** If you suffer from hangovers after drinking wine but not other forms of alcohol, you may be sensitive to sulphur dioxide, a preservative added to wine that is believed to contribute to allergic reactions such as rashes and headaches. Try switching to organic wines, which typically contain, at most, half the sulphur dioxide of non-organic ones.

---

959   **Go topless** Plastics are notoriously difficult to recycle because there are so many different types, which can't be mixed. When putting PET plastic bottles to one side to be recycled, remember to take the caps off, as these are made from a different polymer, and need to be recycled separately.

960 **Don't be a two-fridge household** A surprising number of homes have a second "back-up" fridge or freezer. If you're a chiller-heavy household, think about how much food you really need to keep cool at one time. If you really do need a lot of chilling space, **get one large refrigerator (961)**: this will be cheaper and more efficient to run than two smaller ones. But it's likely that you're actually storing much more food (and cold air) than you really need. Try running down your supplies and making do with just one fridge-freezer, buying fresh food more regularly if necessary. You can always **keep the second fridge in reserve (962)** and just plug it in when the extended family comes for a long stay.

963 **Support your local shops** Many small-scale food retailers go out of business every year in the face of relentless, loss-leading competition from supermarkets. This can create "food deserts" in our town centres. Rather than driving miles to a supermarket, try shopping more regularly at local independent shops – while you still can. You'll help reduce the pollution and congestion generated by trips to out-of-town supermarkets, and give a much-needed boost to your local town or village centre.

964   **The nuclear debate** Nuclear energy
generates almost as much heat among
those who argue about it as it does in our
homes. Its supporters see it as the only
way at present to produce low-carbon
energy on a large scale. They fear that if we
carry on using coal, oil and gas at current rates (or
higher) until renewable sources are capable of meeting our needs,
global warming will have become irreversible in the meantime.

Opponents of nuclear power argue that if we invested as much
in research into new forms of energy as it costs to run nuclear
facilities, renewable energy would soon be widely available. They
believe that we can't justify running the risk of an accident at
– or terrorist attack on – a nuclear power station, because such
an event would be so devastating. Even when a nuclear plant
operates normally, it emits radioactive pollution, which can travel
long distances. Nuclear reactors also produce waste that remains
harmful for thousands of years, causing chronic storage problems.

As a consumer, you can take a stand: **investigate the sources
of your supplier's energy (965)** and change provider if you
don't like what you discover.

966   **Get paid to save the planet**

A growing number of
organizations in almost
every sector now employ
people specifically to help
improve their environmental
performance. If you'd like to reduce
environmental impact from within, consider
applying for one of these posts and use your position to influence
real change. If the organization you currently work for doesn't
have an environmental officer, suggest that it creates such a post
(you may need to suggest that the organization first creates an
environmental policy if it's really behind the times), then submit
your application.

967   **Make powerful pen pals** To have the mandate to make
change happen, decision-makers in government often need to
be able to demonstrate that the electorate wants them to do
something. Provide politicians with the support they need to
make difficult decisions by sending regular postcards advocating
the causes you believe in – whether changes in road-tax

legislation or the scrapping of third-world debt. There may be organized card- or letter-writing campaigns that you can join to amplify your efforts.

968 **Joint venture** Offices waste millions of tonnes of paper each year, yet this material is easily recyclable. There's probably a local or national collection company that will deal with your office waste paper, but if you have difficulties finding one, try setting up a recycling cooperative with other businesses in your area. By talking to your commercial neighbours about recycling, you may even find you can do business with them in other ways. Communication is always good.

969 **Damn fine coffee** Make sure your daily caffeine boost is supplied by coffee beans that have been fairly traded. Once a rarity in the shops, a huge range of Fairtrade coffee is now widely available. In recent years, Fairtrade producer groups have received three times the international price for robusta beans and double the international price for arabicas.

970 **The trouble with farmed fish** You might think that buying farmed fish is a sensible response to the problem of overfishing wild fish (see page 223). However, most fish farms only make things worse. Large-scale, intensive farms plunder huge amounts of wild fish for meal feed (15kg to produce a 3kg farmed salmon), which also denies seals and sea birds their natural food source. Fish kept in high-density pens are vulnerable to disease so they have to be dosed with bucketloads of antibiotics, which can leach into surrounding water and enter the food chain. And when farmed fish escape, as they often do, and breed with their wild counterparts, the natural immunity of the wild population is compromised.

Fortunately, a new breed of fish farmers who recognize the impact that aquaculture can have on the environment is emerging. If you buy farmed fish, **look for fish from low-density, organic farms (971)** that respect the local ecosystem.

972 **Don't get in a lather** Try to avoid using more detergent than you actually need to get your clothes clean. Not only does overdosing waste the resources and energy used to make the detergent, it also makes your washing machine work harder, and requires extra processing to clean up the washing water once it leaves your machine. Follow the dosage instructions on the soap's packaging, and experiment to see whether you can get good results using less (the manufacturer may want you to err on the generous side). You could also **contact your water company to find out how hard or soft your home's water supply is (973)**. Many people overestimate the hardness of their water and end up using far too much detergent.

974 **FAIR PLAY** The Fairtrade movement, most commonly associated with food products such as coffee and bananas, also encompasses toys. Make sure that the producers of your children's playthings have received a fair reward for their labours, and have the chance to enjoy their lives too, by choosing certified Fairtrade toys.

975 **Shades of meaning** Many items are now labelled as "recyclable" with a "mobius loop" triangle of arrows on a light background: ♻. Most things could theoretically be recycled, but buying these products still puts the onus on you to make them available for recycling. Instead, try to choose items made from materials that have already been recycled. These are marked with a mobius loop on a dark background: ♻. A subtle difference on the label with a big impact on the environment.

976 **Blue bottles are no longer a nuisance** Blue bottles (of the glass rather than insect variety) can be recycled in the same system as green ones, so put them in the green container at your local bottle bank.

977 **Red, amber and, above all, green** Many cities, particularly in the USA, are replacing incandescent bulbs in traffic signals with LEDs (see page 345), because they use 80 per cent less electricity. Find out whether your local authority is considering making this switch, and, if not, lobby them to do so. They'll not only save on running costs, but will need to change the bulbs much less often.

978 **Don't shell out for turtle meat** Humans are marine turtles' biggest enemies. Threatened by hunters of their meat, eggs and shells, and by pollution caused by human activity, six out of the world's seven species of marine turtle are at risk of extinction, despite having been protected internationally since 1990. Help these beautiful animals to survive by refusing turtle meat and turtle products if they're ever offered to you as a local delicacy, and support organizations that protect turtle breeding grounds.

---

979 **RECYCLE YOUR CAR** If your old banger is unsaleable, take it to a registered scrapyard for environmentally sound dismantling. Even the most beaten-up wreck probably still contains valuable working parts, and about three-quarters of the material of the car will be recyclable. The majority of this is steel, which can be efficiently and cost-effectively melted down and reused many times over.

---

980 **Curb your can consumption** Seventy-five per cent of the millions of canned drinks sold each day come in aluminium cans. Mining aluminium causes severe environmental damage, then smelting it uses huge amounts of energy: worldwide, the aluminium industry uses as much electric power as the entire African continent. So try to choose drinks in refillable glass bottles. Or, even better, mix your own soft drink in a reusable bottle. If you need to grab a can, make sure you recycle it, as recycling aluminium saves 95 per cent of the energy needed to make a new can.

981   **Kick-start your compost** If you haven't got a garden or your garden's too small for a full-size compost heap, try *bokashi* – a traditional Japanese system for fermenting organic matter to create fertilizer. Its modern incarnation enlists the help of "effective micro-organisms" (EM) to ferment food waste and other organic matter in a speedy "pickling" process. Equip your kitchen with an air-tight *bokashi* bucket. Every time you throw in waste food scraps (including cooked food – even meat and fish), sprinkle in a handful of the EM-infused bran supplied with the bucket, and in a few weeks you'll have nutrient-rich soil improver to dig into your garden (or window-box), and fertilizer juice from the bucket's tap – great for your houseplants.

982 **Rewire without PVC** If your home's due to have its electrical wiring replaced, take advantage of the opportunity to get rid of all the PVC that's likely to be covering it. Polyvinyl chloride (PVC) is the world's second most commonly used and most environmentally harmful plastic. Luckily, it's easy to replace with benign insulating material, so ask your electrician to help detoxify your whole electrical system.

983 **An ocean apart** Europe and North America are divided by more than just the Atlantic – they also have very different approaches to the labelling of genetically modified (GM) foods (see page 337). In the European Union, foods produced with GM ingredients have to be labelled as such, so that consumers can make an informed choice. No such requirement exists in the USA and Canada, the world's biggest producers of GM foods. However, there's a groundswell of opposition to genetic engineering in these countries: a 2003 survey showed that 55 per cent of Americans and 63 per cent of Canadians were against GM foods. If you live in the EU, write to your MEP to **express support for the EU stand against GM foods (984)**. If you're from another part of the world, and would like the opportunity to identify and be able to avoid eating GM food, **contact your local political representative to press for labelling regulations (985)**.

986   **The Great Warming** For a fast-track look at climate change and possible solutions, watch *The Great Warming*. Filmed in eight countries on four continents, endorsed by dozens of the world's leading scientists, this three-hour television series is one of the most factually accurate, visually stunning and wide-ranging productions ever mounted on this complex, fascinating subject.

987 **Chop on a bamboo board**
As an alternative to buying a
chopping board made from tropical
hardwood, look for one made
from bamboo. This fast-growing,
sustainable and versatile material
is extremely durable and naturally
antibacterial, withstands regular
washing, and is a beautiful detail
for your kitchen.

988 **Mail-order happiness** If you can't get the products you need
locally, buying goods online can be an environmentally friendly
and time-saving way to shop. When buying from the cyber-aisles,
try to **plan ahead so that you don't need to demand super-
fast delivery times (989)**. More flexible postal arrangements
allow distributors to run delivery trucks at full capacity and to use
more fuel-efficient forms of transport, such as train and boat. To
save on postage and unnecessary journeys, and to take advantage
of bulk-buy deals, **combine orders with friends, relatives or
colleagues (990)**. If your home is unoccupied for most of the

day, **have orders delivered to your workplace (991)**, where they can always be accepted – this avoids items having to be re-sent, or your having to make awkward and fuel-consuming trips to the delivery depot, if you're not home when they arrive.

992   **COOK SOME MULTI-MEALS** If you're going to the effort of cooking from scratch, try preparing enough for two or three meals, and freezing or refrigerating what you don't want that day (remembering to let the food go cold before you chill it). You may need to chop up a few extra vegetables, but you'll dramatically reduce the amount of energy you and your cooker have to put into the second and third meals – and many foods taste better reheated.

993   **Take the venom out of your rum punch**
Rum is made from sugar cane, which is often heavily sprayed with pesticides. So next time you're rustling up a Caribbean cocktail, use organic rum.

994 Crunch time Lower your breakfast cereal's carbon footprint (see page 17) by dousing it in organic milk, which uses only a third of the energy needed to produce its non-organic counterpart.

995 Everything under one lid Save time and energy in the kitchen by preparing whole meals in one pot. For example, try boiling rice in a large covered pan, then adding a layer of vegetables, plus strips of meat or tofu, and steaming them. Dishes based on potatoes or pasta can be prepared in a similar way, as can traditional stews and pot roasts. Whatever the recipe, a one-pot meal will generally use about a third of the energy of a meal cooked in separate pans.

996 Medicinal effect If you've bought or been prescribed medicine that you no longer need, rather than leaving it to fester in your bathroom cabinet until you clear it into the bin, pass it on to a humanitarian organization that can redistribute it to some of the thousands of people who die every day because they don't have access to proper medical care.

997 Face-to-face shopping Before supermarkets, shopping used to be a far more sociable experience. Rediscover the friendlier way to shop by buying your groceries over the counter from specialist food shops – or, failing that, from the deli counter at your supermarket. That way, you can ask for exactly the amount that you need, making it less likely that food will go to waste, and bypass the hermetically sealed plastic packaging to be found in the aisles.

998 Back-door GMOs If you want to avoid eating genetically modified organisms (GMOs), you can look for food that is labelled GMO-free (see page 360) or certified organic. But if you eat meat or animal products, you may be eating GMOs unknowingly, as there's currently no requirement anywhere in the world to label products from animals that have been fed on GM feed. If you don't want to be exposed to GM crops by this indirect route, write to farmers and food distributors asking them to keep GM crops out of animal feed.

999 **Celebrate a cigarette-free life** If you manage to give up smoking, celebrate by planting a tree every year on the anniversary of your last puff – or have one planted on your behalf (see page 65). Each year, 200,000 hectares of woodland are destroyed to make way for tobacco plantations. Now that your lungs are getting cleaner, it's time to return the favour by helping to replenish the planet's lungs.

1000 **Quick thinkers avoid fast-food** When you're on the go in an unfamiliar area, it can be hard to find somewhere healthy to eat, particularly if you've got hungry children in tow, with their finely tuned pester powers. Try to avoid succumbing to the ubiquitous junk-fuel stations by keeping a supply of healthy snacks in your bag, such as mixed nuts, seeds and dried fruit, to stave off hunger pangs for long enough to find a place that'll serve you a decent meal. You'll avoid the intensively and pollutingly mass-produced food served by fast-food chains and the mountains of non-recyclable packaging they produce. And you and the environment will be healthier for it.

1001 **Sail into the sunset** Capturing the wind's energy in a sail is a wonderfully low-impact way of getting around. If you don't happen to own your own yacht, you can still explore the oceans on a zero-carbon vessel by helping to crew a sailing boat. Scour ads in sailing magazines for opportunities, and get ready to head for the Bahamas. (It might be a good idea to have a few sailing lessons first!)

FURTHER READING

Christensen, K. *The Armchair Environmentalist*. MQ Publications, 2004.

Clark, D. *The Rough Guide to Ethical Shopping*. Rough Guides, 2004.

Drake, J. and Love, A. *The Kids' Summer Games Book*. Kids Can Press, 2002.

Duncanson, A. *Ecology Begins at Home*. Green Books, 2004.

Hacker, R. *How to Live Green, Cheap and Happy*. Stackpole Books, 1994.

Hickman, L. *A Good Life*. Transworld Publishers, 2005.

Khaneka, P. *Do the Right Things*. New Internationalist Publications, 2004.

Lawrence, F. *Not on the Label*. Penguin Books, 2004.

Milord, S. *The Kids' Nature Book*. Williamson, 1996.

Petrini, C. *Slow Food*. Columbia University Press, 2001.

Reay, D. *Climate Change Begins at Home*. Macmillan, 2005.

Scott, N. *Composting*. Green Books, 2006.

Sullivan, K. *Organic Living in 10 Simple Lessons*. Barron's Educational Series, 2001.

Various authors. *Recycle*. Black Dog Publishing, 2006.

Worldwatch Institute. *Vital Signs*. Norton, published annually.

Young, W. *Sold Out – The True Cost of Supermarket Shopping*. Vision Paperbacks, 2004.

USEFUL WEBSITES

General information

Common Ground (www.commonground.org.uk)

Creative Environmental Networks (www.cen.org.uk)

The Ecologist online magazine (www.theecologist.org)

Friends of the Earth (www.foe.co.uk)

Global Action Plan (www.globalactionplan.org.uk)

Greenpeace (www.greenpeace.org.uk)

Worldwatch Institute (www.worldwatch.org)

Babies and children

BabyGROE (www.babygroe.co.uk)

Eco-Schools (www.eco-schools.org.uk)

Institute for Earth Education (www.eartheducation.org). *Learning resources.*

La Leche League GB (www.laleche.org.uk). *Breastfeeding.*

National Association of Toy and Leisure Libraries (www.natll.org.uk)

Wastefreelunches.org (www.wastefreelunches.org)

Women's Environmental Network (www.wen.org.uk). *Reusable nappies.*

Biodiversity and ecology

British Beekeepers Association (www.bbka.org.uk)

British Trust for Conservation Volunteers (www.btcv.org.uk)

Convention on International Trade in Endangered Species of Wild Fauna and Flora
   (www.cites.org)
Earthwatch Institute (www.earthwatch.org)
Forest Stewardship Council (www.fsc.org)
Global Trees Campaign (www.globaltrees.org)
Rainforest Foundation (www.rainforestfoundationuk.org)
Royal Society for the Protection of Birds (www.rspb.org.uk). *Advice on feeding birds*
Trees for Cities (www.treesforcities.org)
Trust for Urban Ecology (www.urbanecology.org.uk). *Volunteer to take part in environmental projects.*
Wildlife Trusts (www.wildlifetrusts.org.uk)
World Land Trust (www.worldlandtrust.org). *Buy a section of rainforest.*
World Society for the Protection of Animals (www.wspa.org.uk)

Climate change
Carbon Footprint (www.carbonfootprint.com)
Carbon Neutral Company (www.carbonneutral.com)
Earth Day Network (www.earthday.net). *Includes Ecological Footprint Quiz.*
Nature's Calendar (www.naturescalendar.org.uk). *Report phenological events.*

Consumer and shopping
Environmental Working Group (www.ewg.org). *Includes guide to ingredients of cosmetics and toiletries.*

Ethical Junction (www.ethical-junction.org)

Fairtrade Foundation (www.fairtrade.org.uk)

Freecycle (www.freecycle.org)

Good Shopping Guide (www.thegoodshoppingguide.co.uk)

GreenChoices (www.greenchoices.org)

Green Consumer Guide (www.greenconsumerguide.com)

Green Guide (www.greenguide.co.uk)

Gumtree (www.gumtree.co.uk). *Includes listings of second-hand items for sale.*

Local Exchange Trading Systems (www.lets-linkup.com).
Find a LETS group near you.

Energy

Alliance to Save Energy (www.ase.org)

Ban the Bulb (www.banthebulb.org). *Low-energy lighting.*

Centre for Alternative Technology (www.cat.org.uk)

Eartheasy (www.eartheasy.com)

Energy Saving Trust (www.est.org.uk)

Good Energy (www.good-energy.co.uk). *Change to a green electricity tariff.*

National Energy Foundation (www.nef.org.uk)

Ethical living

Ethical Investment Research Services (www.eiris.org)

Ethical Wills (www.ethicalwill.com)

Food and drink

Compassion in World Farming (www.ciwf.org)

CSA Cultivating Communities (www.cuco.org.uk)

Marine Stewardship Council (www.msc.org). *Search for sustainable seafood.*

Soil Association (www.soilassociation.org)

Sustain (www.sustainweb.org). *Better food and farming.*

Leisure

Organic Places to Stay (www.organicholidays.com)

Pioneer Thinking (www.pioneerthinking.com). *Craft techniques, including making paper.*

Reed Design (www.reeddesign.co.uk). *Make your own kite.*

Ski Club of Great Britain (www.skiclub.co.uk). *Includes Green Resort Guide.*

Vegetarian Vacations (www.vegetarian-vacations.com)

Low-impact living

Eekos (www.eekos.com). *Information resource for sustainable living.*

Global Eco-village Network (www.ecovillage.org)

Green Builder (www.greenbuilder.co.uk). *Search for green architects, builders and building materials.*

Low-Impact Living Initiative (www.lowimpact.org)

Voluntary Simplicity (www.theworld.com/ ~ habib/thegarden//simplicity/)

Woodsmoke (www.woodsmoke.uk.com). *Bushcraft techniques.*

Travel and transport

CarSharing.net (www.carsharing.net). *Car clubs and car-share schemes.*

Climate Care (www.climatecare.org). *Calculate and buy carbon offsets.*

Cyclists' Touring Club (www.ctc.org.uk)

Global Stewards (www.globalstewards.org/hotel.htm). *List of environmental tips for hotels.*

Green Hotels Association (www.greenhotels.com)

Man in Seat 61 (www.seat61.com). *Plan flight-free journeys.*

Ramblers' Association (www.ramblers.org.uk)

Sustrans (www.sustrans.org.uk). *Sustainable transport.*

Travellers' Alert (www.bornfree.org.uk/travellers.alert). *Report animal cruelty while abroad.*

Waste

Abebooks (www.abebooks.co.uk). *Search for second-hand books.*

Mail Preference Service (www.mpsonline.org.uk). *Opt out of junk mail.*

Re-Cycle (www.re-cycle.org). *Send second-hand bicycles to Africa.*

Title Trader (www.titletrader.com). *Swap books, DVDs and CDs.*

Waste and Resources Action Programme (www.wrap.org.uk)

Water

Surfers Against Sewage (www.sas.org.uk)

Xeriscape (www.xeriscape.org). *Low-water gardening.*

INDEX

ABOUT THE AUTHOR

Joanna Yarrow is a director of the environmental consultancy Beyond Green Ltd.
She helps individuals and corporations create action plans for eco-friendly living.

ACKNOWLEDGMENTS

Page 315: quotation from *Eco-Economy* by Lester R. Brown (Earthscan, 2001).
Copyright © Earth Policy Institute.